occam® 2
REFERENCE MANUAL

Prentice Hall International
Series in Computer Science

C.A.R. Hoare, Series Editor

BACKHOUSE, R.C., *Program Construction and Verification*
BACKHOUSE, R.C., *Syntax of Programming Languages: theory and practice*
DE BAKKER, J.W., *Mathematical Theory of Program Correctness*
BJÖRNER, D., and JONES, C.B., *Formal Specification and Software Development*
BORNAT, R., *Programming from First Principles*
BUSTARD, D., ELDER, J., and WELSH, J., *Concurrent Program Structures*
CLARK, K.L., and McCABE, F.G., *micro-Prolog: programming in logic*
DROMEY, R.G., *How to Solve it by Computer*
DUNCAN, F., *Microprocessor Programming and Software Development*
ELDER, J., *Construction of Data Processing Software*
GOLDSCHLAGER, L., and LISTER, A., *Computer Science: a modern introduction*
HAYES, I. (ed.), *Specification Case Studies*
HEHNER, E.C.R., *The Logic of Programming*
HENDERSON, P., *Functional Programming: application and implementation*
HOARE, C.A.R., *Communicating Sequential Processes*
HOARE, C.A.R., and SHEPHERDSON, J.C. (eds), *Mathematical Logic and Programming Languages*
INMOS LTD, *occam Programming Manual*
INMOS LTD, *occam 2 Reference Manual*
JACKSON, M.A., *System Development*
JOHNSTON, H., *Learning to Program*
JONES, C.B., *Systematic Software Development using VDM*
JONES, G., *Programming in occam*
JOSEPH, M., PRASAD, V.R., and NATARAJAN, N., *A Multiprocessor Operating System*
LEW, A., *Computer Science: a mathematical introduction*
MacCALLUM, I., *Pascal for the Apple*
MacCALLUM, I., *UCSD Pascal for the IBM PC*
PEYTON JONES, S.L., *The Implementation of Functional Programming Languages*
POMBERGER, G., *Software Engineering and Modula-2*
REYNOLDS, J.C., *The Craft of Programming*
SLOMAN, M., and KRAMER, J., *Distributed Systems and Computer Networks*
TENNENT, R.D., *Principles of Programming Languages*
WATT. D.A., WICHMANN, B.A., and FINDLAY, W., *ADA: language and methodology*
WELSH, J., and ELDER, J., *Introduction to Modula-2*
WELSH, J., and ELDER, J., *Introduction to Pascal (2nd edn)*
WELSH, J., ELDER, J., and BUSTARD, D., *Sequential Program Structures*
WELSH, J., and HAY, A., *A Model Implementation of Standard Pascal*
WELSH, J., and McKEAG, M., *Structured System Programming*
WIKSTRÖM, Å., *Functional Programming using Standard ML*

occam® 2
REFERENCE MANUAL

INMOS Limited

PRENTICE HALL

NEW YORK   LONDON   TORONTO   SYDNEY   TOKYO   SINGAPORE

First published 1988 by
Prentice Hall International (UK) Ltd,
66 Wood Land End, Hemel Hempstead,
Hertfordshire, HP2 4RG
A division of
Simon & Schuster International Group

INMOS logo, **inmos,** IMS and occam are registered
trademarks of the INMOS Group of Companies.

INMOS document number: 72 occ 45 02

Printed and bound in Great Britain at the University
Press, Cambridge.

CIP data are available.

4 5 6 7   93 92 91 90

ISBN 0-13-629312-3

Contents

Contents overview

The preliminaries

Preface	A few words about the language.
Introduction	A few words about the book.
Syntax and program format	Describes the modified BNF used in occam syntax, and details program format and annotation.

The chapters

The appendices

Preface

The occam programming language is a high level language, designed to express concurrent algorithms and their implementation on a network of processing components.

The occam *reference manual* serves to provide a single reference, and definition of the language occam. The manual describes each aspect of the language, starting with the most primitive components of an occam program, and moving on to cover the whole language in detail. The manual is addressed to the wider audience, including not only the computer scientist, software engineer and programmer, but also the electronics engineer and system designer.

Programming in occam is easy. occam enables an application to be described as a collection of *processes*, where each process executes concurrently, and communicates with other processes through *channels*. Each process in such an application describes the behaviour of a particular aspect of the implementation, and each channel describes the connection between each of the processes. This approach has two important consequences. Firstly, it gives the program a clearly defined and simple structure. Secondly, it allows the application to exploit the performance of a system which consists of many parts.

Concurrency and communication are the prime concepts of the occam model. occam captures the hierarchical structure of a system by allowing an interconnected set of processes to be regarded as a unified, single process. At any level of detail, the programmer is only concerned with a small, manageable set of processes.

occam is an ideal introduction to a number of key methodologies in modern computer science. occam programs can provide a degree of security unknown in conventional programming languages such as C, FORTRAN or Pascal. occam simplifies the task of program verification, by allowing application of mathematical proof techniques to prove the correctness of programs. Transformations, which convert a process from one form to a directly equivalent form, can be applied to the source of an occam program to improve its efficiency in any particular environment. occam makes an ideal language for specification and behavioural description. occam programs are easily configured onto the hardware of a system or indeed, may specify the hardware of a system.

The founding principle of occam is a minimalist approach which avoids unnecessary duplication of language mechanism, and is named after the 14th century philosopher William of Occam who proposed that invented entities should not be duplicated beyond necessity. This proposition has become known as "Occam's razor".

The occam programming language arises from the concepts founded by David May in EPL (Experimental Programming Language) and Tony Hoare in CSP.(Communicating Sequential Processes). Since its conception in 1982 occam has been, and continues to be under development at INMOS Ltd, in the United Kingdom, under the direction of David May. The development of the INMOS transputer, a device which places a microcomputer on a single chip, has been closely related to occam, its design and implementation. The transputer reflects the occam architectural model, and may be considered an occam machine. occam is the language of the transputer and as such, when used to program a single transputer or a network of transputers, provides the equivalent efficiency to programming a conventional computer at assembler level. However, this manual does not make any assumptions about the hardware implementation of the language or the target system.

occam is a trademark of the INMOS group of companies.

Introduction

This manual describes the programming language occam 2, which differs in a number of ways from the prototype language occam 1. The prototype language gave programmers and designers an early introduction to the concepts of concurrency in programming and design. occam 2 introduces a number of new aspects to the language that extend both its use and facility. In particular, occam 2 introduces floating point representation of real numbers, functions and a data typing system.

This manual was completed during 1986 and 1987 as a part of the final development of occam 2 at the INMOS Microcomputer Centre, Bristol, UK..

Using this manual

This book is designed primarily to be used as a reference text for the programming language occam. However, the manual should also serve as an introduction to the language for someone with a reasonable understanding of programming languages. The primitive aspects of the language are presented at the start of the manual, with as few forward references as possible. It is therefore possible to read the manual from cover to cover, giving the reader an insight into the language as a whole. The manual is cross referenced throughout, and a full index and glossary of terms are provided at the end of the manual.

Keywords and example program fragments appear in a **bold program font** throughout, for example:

```
-- example program fragment
IF
  occam
    programming := easy
```

Words which appear in *italic* indicate a syntactic object, but may also serve to emphasise a need to cross reference and encourage referral to the index. Mathematical symbols and names referring to a mathematical values use a *roman italic font*.

Figures are used in a number of places to illustrate examples, they use the following conventions: an arrowed line represents a *channel*, a round cornered box represents a *process* (refered to here as a *process box*), a lighter coloured process box combines a number of smaller processes. The conventions are illustrated in figure I.1.

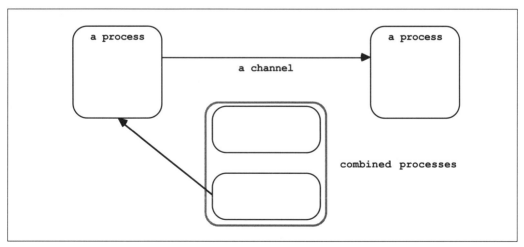

Figure I.1 Figure conventions

Syntax and program format

Syntactic notation

The syntax of OCCam programs is described in a modified Backus-Naur Form (BNF). As an example, the following shows the syntax of *assignment*, discussed on page 5:

    assignment =   *variable* := *expression*

This means "An assignment is a *variable* followed by the symbol := , followed by an *expression*". A vertical bar (|) means "or", so for example:

action =	*assignment*		*action* =	*assignment*
|	*input*	is the same as	*action* =	*input*
|	*output*		*action* =	*output*

The meaning of this syntax is "An action is an *assignment*, an *input*, or an *output*".

The written structure of OCCam programs is specified by the syntax. Each statement in an OCCam program normally occupies a single line, and the indentation of each statement forms an intrinsic part of the syntax of the language. The following example shows the syntax for *sequence* discussed on page 9:

    sequence =   SEQ
                   { *process* }

The syntax here means "A sequence is the keyword **SEQ** followed by zero or more processes, each on a separate line, and indented two spaces beyond **SEQ**". Curly brackets { and } are used to indicate the number of times some syntactic object occurs. { *process* } means, "zero or more processes, each on a separate line". Similarly, {$_0$, *expression* }, means "A list of zero or more expressions, separated by commas", and {$_1$, *expression* }, means "A list of one or more expressions, separated by commas".

A complete summary of the syntax of the language is given at the end of the main body of the manual (starting on page 80).

Continuation lines

A long statement may be broken immediately after one of the following:

an operator	i.e. +, -, *, / etc..
a comma	,
a semi-colon	;
assignment	:=
the keyword	**IS**, **FROM** or **FOR**

A statement can be broken over several lines providing the continuation is indented at least as much as the first line of the statement.

The annotation of occam programs

As the format of OCCam programs is significant, there are a number of rules concerning how programs are annotated. A comment is introduced by a double dash symbol (--), and extends to the end of the line.

Consider the following sequence:

```
SEQ
    -- This example illustrates the use of comments
    -- A comment may not be indented less than
        --       the following statement
    ...
    SEQ        -- A sequence
    ...
```

Comments may not be indented less than the following statement.

Names and keywords used in occam programs

Names used in occam programs must begin with an alphabetic character. Names consist of a sequence of alphanumeric characters and dots. There is no length restriction. occam is sensitive to the case of names, i.e. **Say** is considered different from **say**. With the exception of the names of channels protocols, names in the examples presented in this manual are all lower case. However, the following are all valid names in occam:

```
PACKETS
vector6
LinkOut
NOT.A.NUMBER
transputer
terminal.in
terminalOut
```

All keywords are upper case (e.g. **SEQ**). All keywords are reserved, and thus may not be used by the programmer. A full list of the keywords appear on page 91. The names of library routines are given in the appendix starting on page 94.

1 Primitive processes

1.1 Assignment

occam programs are built from processes. The simplest process in an occam program is an *action*. An action is either an *assignment*, an *input* or an *output*. Consider the following example:

```
x := y + 2
```

This simple example is an *assignment*, which assigns the value of the expression y + 2 to the variable x. The syntax of an assignment is:

assignment = *variable* := *expression*

The *variable* on the left of the assignment symbol (:=) is assigned the value of the *expression* on the right of the symbol. The value of the expression must be of the same *data type* as the variable to which it is to be assigned, otherwise the assignment is not valid.

Variables are discussed on page 26, data types are discussed on page 23, and expressions on page 43.

A multiple assignment assigns values to several variables, as illustrated in the following example:

```
a, b, c := x, y + 1, z + 2
```

This assignment assigns the values of x, y + 1 and z + 2 to the variables a, b and c respectively. The expressions on the right of the assignment are evaluated, and the assignments are then performed in parallel. Consider the following example:

```
x, y := y, x
```

The effect of this multiple assignment is to swap the values of the variables x and y.

The syntax of multiple assignment extends the syntax for assignment:

assignment = *variable.list* := *expression.list*
variable.list = {$_1$, *variable* }
expression.list = {$_1$, *expression* }

A list of expressions appearing to the right of the assignment symbol (:=) are evaluated in parallel, and then each value is assigned (in parallel) to the corresponding variable of the list to the left of the symbol. The rules which govern the names used in a multiple assignment therefore follow from those for names used in parallel constructions (see page 54). Practically, this means that no name may appear twice on the left side of a multiple assignment, as the name of a variable or as the name of a variable and the name of a subscript expression which selects a component from an array (arrays are explained in chapter 6 which starts on page 39).

The expression on the right of the assignment symbol (:=) may be a function. A multiple result function can be an expression list in a multiple assignment. Functions are discussed in chapter 11 starting on page 65.

1.2   Communication

Communication is an essential part of occam programming. Values are passed between concurrent processes by communication on *channels*. Each channel provides unbuffered, unidirectional point-to-point communication between two concurrent processes. The format and *type* of communication on a channel is
specified by a *channel protocol* given in the *declaration* of a channel. Channel protocols are discussed in
chapter 4, which starts on page 29, and channel declarations are discussed in the same chapter on page 29.

Two *actions* exist in occam which perform communication on a channel. They are: *input* and *output*.

1.2.1   Input

An *input* receives a value from a *channel* and assigns the received value to a *variable*. Consider the following
example:

keyboard ? char

This simple example receives a value from the channel named **keyboard** and assigns the value to the
variable **char**. The input waits until a value is received.

The syntax of an input is:

input   =   *channel* ? *variable*

An input receives a value from the channel on the left of the input symbol (?), and assigns that value to
the variable on the right of the symbol. The value input must be of the same *data type* as the variable to
which it is assigned, otherwise the input is not valid. Variables are discussed on page 26, and data types are
discussed on page 23.

1.2.2   Output

An *output* transmits the value of an *expression* to a *channel*. Consider the following example:

screen ! char

This simple example transmits the value of the variable **char** to the channel named **screen**. The output
waits until the value has been received by a corresponding input.

The syntax of an output is:

output   =   *channel* ! *expression*

An output transmits the value of the expression on the right of the output symbol (!) to the channel named
on the left of the symbol.

Variables are discussed on page 26 and expressions on page 43.

1.3   SKIP and STOP

The primitive process **SKIP** starts, performs no action and terminates.

The primitive process **STOP** starts, performs no action and never terminates.

To explain how **SKIP** behaves, consider the following *sequence*:

```
SEQ
   keyboard ? char
   SKIP
   screen   ! char
```

This sequence executes the input **keyboard ? char**, then executes **SKIP**, which performs no action. The sequence continues, and the output **screen ! char** is executed. The behaviour of **STOP** is illustrated by the following sequence:

```
SEQ
   keyboard ? char
   STOP
   screen   ! char
```

This sequence performs the input **keyboard ? char** before, then executes **STOP**, which starts but does not terminate and so does not allow the sequence to continue. The output **screen ! char** is never executed.

2 Combining processes

occam programs are built from processes. Primitive processes are described in the previous chapter. Larger processes are built by combining smaller processes in a *construction*. A construction builds a process of one of the following kind:

SEQ	sequence
IF	conditional
CASE	selection
WHILE	loop
PAR	parallel
ALT	alternation

A sequential process is built by combining processes in a sequence, conditional or selection construction. A loop is built by combining processes in a **WHILE** loop. Concurrent processes are built with parallel and alternation constructions, and communicate using channels, inputs and outputs.

The constructions **SEQ**, **IF**, **PAR** and **ALT** can all be *replicated*. A replicated construction *replicates* the constructed *process*, *choice* or *alternative* a specified number of times. Details of replication applied to each of these constructions is given in the following sections.

2.1   Sequence

A sequence combines processes into a construction in which one process follows another. Consider the following example:

```
SEQ
    keyboard ? char
    screen   ! char
```

This process combines two actions which are performed sequentially. The input **keyboard ? char** receives a value which is assigned to the variable **char**, then the following output **screen ! char** is performed.

Programs are built by constructing larger processes from smaller ones. Thus a construction may contain other constructions, as shown in the following example:

```
SEQ
  SEQ
    screen ! '?'
    keyboard ? char
  SEQ
    screen ! char
    screen ! cr
    screen ! lf
```

This simple example combines five actions, and suggests how embedded sequences may be used to show the hierarchical structure of a program. Embedding constructions of the same kind has no effect on the behaviour of the process. This example is equivalent to the following:

```
SEQ
    screen ! '?'
    keyboard ? char
    screen ! char
    screen ! cr
    screen ! lf
```

The syntax for a sequence is:

```
sequence  =   SEQ
                { process }
```

The keyword **SEQ** is followed by zero or more processes at an indentation of two spaces.

2.1.1   Replicated sequence

A sequence can be *replicated* to produce a number of similar processes which are performed in sequence, and behave like a conventional counted loop. Consider the following:

```
SEQ i = 0 FOR array.size
  stream ! data.array[i]
```

This process performs the output **stream ! data.array[i]** the number of times specified by the value of **array.size**. The initial value of the *index* **i** is specified by a base value (in this case 0). In the above sequence the value of **i** for the first output is 0, and for each successive output performed the value of the index is an increment of its previous value. If **array.size** has the value 2, the example can be expanded to show the effect of the replication as follows:

```
SEQ
  stream ! data.array[0]
  stream ! data.array[1]
```

Consider the following example in which the base value is 14:

```
SEQ i = 14 FOR 2
  stream ! data.array[i]
```

This example may also be expanded to show the value of the index for each replication, as follows:

```
SEQ
  stream ! data.array[14]
  stream ! data.array[15]
```

This example uses an *array*; arrays (page 39) are explained later in the manual.

The syntax for a replicated sequence extends the syntax for sequences:

```
sequence   =   SEQ replicator
                 process
replicator =   name = base FOR count
base       =   expression
count      =   expression
```


The keyword **SEQ** and a replicator are followed by a process which is indented two spaces. The replicator appears to the right of the keyword **SEQ**. The replicator specifies a name for the index (i.e. the name does not need to be declared elsewhere). The value of the index for the first replication is the value of the *base* expression, and the number of times the process is replicated is the value of the *count* expression at the start of the sequence.

The index may be used in expressions but cannot be assigned to by an input or assignment. The index has a value of *type* **INT**. The base and count expressions must also be of data type **INT**. Data types (page 23) are explained later in the the manual. A negative value count expression is *invalid*. See appendix E, page 78 for an explanation of how *invalid processes* behave. If the value of the count expression is zero, the replicated sequence behaves like the primitive process **SKIP** (page 7).

2.2   Conditional

A conditional combines a number of processes each of which is guarded by a boolean expression. The conditional evaluates each boolean expression in sequence; if a boolean expression is found to be true the associated process is performed, and the conditional terminates. If none of the boolean expressions are true the conditional behaves like the primitive process **STOP** (page 7), for example:

```
IF
  x < y
    x := x + 1
  x >= y
    SKIP
```

Consider this example in detail: if $x < y$ is true, the associated process $x := x + 1$ is performed, however if the expression $x < y$ is false, the next boolean expression $x >= y$ is evaluated. If $x >= y$ is true, then the associated process **SKIP** is performed. In this example, one of the boolean expressions must be true. However, consider the next example:

```
IF
  x < y
    x := x + 1
```

This conditional has a single component. If the expression $x < y$ is false then the conditional will behave like the primitive process **STOP** (page 7). It is often convenient to use a form of conditional where the final choice is guaranteed to be performed, as illustrated by the following example:

```
IF
  x > y
    order := gt
  x < y
    order := lt
  TRUE
    order := eq
```

The expressions $x > y$ and $x < y$ will each be either true or false. The final expression uses the boolean constant **TRUE** which is always true, and acts as a catch-all which causes the associated process to be performed if none of the previous boolean expressions are true. In this context **TRUE** may be read as "otherwise".

The syntax for a conditional is:

```
conditional       =   IF
                        { choice }
choice            =   guarded.choice | conditional
guarded.choice    =   boolean
                        process
boolean           =   expression
```

The keyword **IF** is followed by zero or more choices, indented two spaces. A choice is either a *guarded* choice or another conditional. A guarded choice is a boolean expression followed by a process, indented two spaces.

A choice which is itself a conditional has the same behaviour if "flattened out" in a similar way to the embedded sequences shown earlier (page 9). Consider the following example:

```
IF
  IF
    x > y
      x := x + 1
  TRUE
    SKIP
```

This has the same effect as:

```
IF
    x > y
        x := x + 1
    TRUE
        SKIP
```

Boolean expressions (page 48) are discussed later in the manual.

2.2.1   Replicated conditional

A conditional may also be replicated, just as a sequence may (page 10). A replicated conditional constructs a number of similar choices. The following example compares the two strings **string** and **object**:

```
IF
    IF i = 1 FOR length
        string[i] <> object[i]
            found := FALSE
    TRUE
        found := TRUE
```

The first choice in this example is a replicated conditional. This has created a number of similar choices each guarded by a boolean expression comparing a component of the array **string** and the array **object**. The replication may be expanded to show its meaning. If **length** has a constant value 2, this example has the same effect as:

```
IF
    IF
        string[1] <> object[1]
            found := FALSE
        string[2] <> object[2]
            found := FALSE
    TRUE
        found := TRUE
```

or

```
IF
    IF
        string[1] <> object[1]
            found := FALSE
        string[2] <> object[2]
            found := FALSE
    TRUE
        found := TRUE
```

The syntax for the replicated conditional is:

conditional	=	**IF** *replicator*
		choice
replicator	=	*name* = *base* **FOR** *count*
base	=	*expression*
count	=	*expression*

The keyword **IF** and a replicator are followed by a choice which is indented two spaces. The replicator appears to the right of the keyword **IF**. The replicator specifies a name for the index. The value of the index for the first replication is the value of the *base* expression, and the number of times the choice is replicated is the value of the *count* expression.

The index may be used in expressions but cannot be assigned to by an input or assignment. The index is of *data type* **INT**. The data type of the base and the count expressions must also be of type **INT**. Data types (page 23) are explained later in the the manual. A negative value count expression is *invalid*. See appendix E, page 78 for an explanation of how *invalid processes* behave. If the value of the count expression is zero, the replicated conditional behaves like the primitive process **STOP** (page 7).

2.3   Selection

A selection combines a number of *options*, one of which is selected by matching the value of a *selector* with the value of a constant expression (called a *case expression*) associated with the option. Consider the following example:

```
CASE direction
  up
    x := x + 1
  down
    x := x - 1
```

In this example the value of **direction** is compared to the value of the case expressions **up** and **down**. If **direction** has a value equal to **up** then **x** := **x** + 1 is performed, if **direction** has a value equal to **down** then **x** := **x** - 1 is performed, however if no match is found, the selection behaves like the primitive process **STOP** (page 7). Several case expressions may be associated with a single option, for example:

```
CASE letter
  'a', 'e', 'i', 'o', 'u'
    vowel := TRUE
```

If **letter** has the value `'a'`, `'e'`, `'i'`, `'o'`, or `'u'`, then the variable **vowel** is assigned the value **TRUE**, otherwise the selection behaves like the primitive process **STOP**. Here it is useful to use a special form of selection where one of the *options* is guaranteed to be performed, as illustrated below:

```
CASE letter
  'a', 'e', 'i', 'o', 'u'
    vowel := TRUE
  ELSE
    vowel := FALSE
```

The process associated with **ELSE** in a selection will be performed if none of the case expressions match the selector.

The syntax for a selection is:

selection	=	**CASE** *selector*
		{ *option* }
option	=	{₁ , *case.expression* }
		process
	|	**ELSE**
		process
selector	=	*expression*
case.expression	=	*expression*

The keyword **CASE** is followed by zero or more *options*, indented two spaces. An option starts with either a list of case expressions or the keyword **ELSE**. This is followed by a process, indented two spaces. All case expressions used in a selection must have distinct constant values (that is, each must be a different value from the other expressions used). The selector and the case expressions must be the same data type, which may be either an integer or a byte data type. A selection can have only one **ELSE** option.

Constant expressions may be given a name in an *abbreviation* (page 57). Data types (page 23) and expressions (page 43) are also discussed later.

2.4   Loop

A loop repeats a process while an associated *boolean expression* is true. Consider the following example:

```
WHILE buffer <> eof
  SEQ
      in  ? buffer
      out ! buffer
```

This loop repeatedly copies a value from the channel **in** to the channel **out**. The copying continues while the boolean expression **buffer <> eof** is true. The sequence is not performed if the boolean expression is initially false.

To further illustrate how processes combine, consider the following process:

```
SEQ
    -- initialise variables
    pointer  := 0
    finished := FALSE
    found    := FALSE
    -- search until found or end of string
    WHILE NOT finished
      IF
        string[pointer] <> char
          IF
            pointer < end.of.string
              pointer := pointer + 1
            pointer = end.of.string
              finished := TRUE
        string[pointer] = char
          SEQ
            found    := TRUE
            finished := TRUE
```

This example searches the array **string** for a character (**char**). Note how the process is built from primitive processes and constructions. In fact it is simpler and easier to write this example using a replicated conditional (page 12) as follows:

```
IF
    IF i = 0 FOR string.size
      string[i] = char
        found := TRUE
    TRUE
      found := FALSE
```

The syntax for a loop is:

```
loop    =  WHILE boolean
              process
boolean =  expression
```

The keyword **WHILE** and a boolean expression are followed by a process which is indented two spaces. The boolean expression appears to the right of the keyword **WHILE**.

2.5   Parallel

The parallel is one of the most useful constructs of the occam language. A parallel combines a number of processes which are performed concurrently. Consider the following example:

```
PAR
  editor    (term.in, term.out)
  keyboard  (term.in)
  screen    (term.out)
```

This parallel combines three named processes (known as procedures, page 61), which are performed to-gether. They start together and terminate when all three processes have terminated. The editor and key-board process communicate using channel **term.in**, the screen and editor communicate using channel **term.out**.

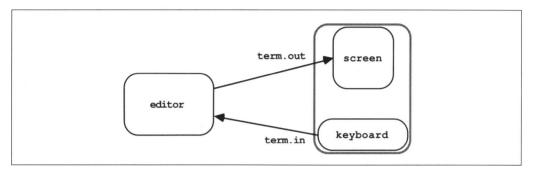

Figure 2.1 Communicating concurrent processes

Values are passed between concurrent processes by communication on *channels* (page 29) using input and output (page 6). Each channel provides unbuffered unidirectional point-to-point communication between two concurrent processes. Figure 2.1 illustrates the channels connecting the three processes in the above example.

The example above shows the parallel being used to tie together the major components of a system. However, a parallel may also be used simply to allow communication and computation to proceed together, as in the following example:

```
WHILE next <> eof
  SEQ
    x := next
    PAR
      in  ? next
      out ! x * x
```

The parallel in this example inputs the next value to be processed from one channel while the last value is being processed and output on another.

The syntax of a parallel is similar to that of a sequence:

parallel =   **PAR**
                  { *process* }

The keyword **PAR** is followed by zero or more processes at an indentation of two spaces.

Parallels may be nested to form the hierarchical structure of a program. The behaviour of the following process is the same as the earlier example:

```
PAR
    editor (term.in, term.out)
    PAR
        keyboard (term.in)
        screen    (term.out)
```

Writing a parallel like this helps later in program development when a program must be *configured* to its environment (when its processes are allocated to physical devices).

A parallel construction which specifies a priority of execution on a single processing device able to perform several tasks (i.e. a multi-tasking processor) is described in appendix A.2.1, page 71.

Rules concerning the use of names in parallels are given in chapter 8 on scope starting on page 53, and are summarised in the appendix (page 75).

2.5.1   Replicated parallel

A parallel can be replicated, in the same way as sequences and conditionals described earlier. A replicated parallel constructs a number of similar concurrent processes, as shown in the following example:

```
PAR i = 3 FOR 4
    user[i] ! message
```

This replication performs the four outputs concurrently, and is equivalent to

```
PAR
    user[3] ! message
    user[4] ! message
    user[5] ! message
    user[6] ! message
```

Now consider the following example:

```
PAR
    farmer ()
    PAR i = 0 FOR 4
        worker (i)
```

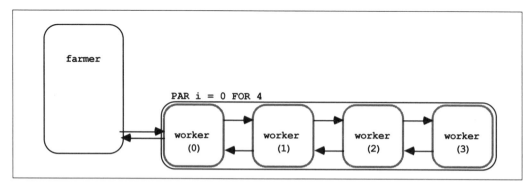

Figure 2.2 A farm of parallel processes

The replicated parallel in this example starts 4 processes, each a copy of the procedure **worker**, and terminates when all four processes are finished. Figure 2.2 shows the structure of this process, which is elaborated upon in the following section. Unlike sequence and conditional replications, the *base* and *count* values (here 0 and 4) must be constant. The procedure **worker** takes a single *parameter* (page 61), for each *instance* (page 61) of the procedure the value of the index **i** is passed. Expanding the replication shows that the above example is equivalent to the following:

```
PAR
  farmer ()
  PAR
    worker (0)
    worker (1)
    worker (2)
    worker (3)
```

The syntax of a replicated parallel is similar to that of the replicated sequence shown earlier in the manual:

parallel	=	**PAR** *replicator*
		process
replicator	=	*name = base* **FOR** *count*
base	=	*expression*
count	=	*expression*

The keyword **PAR** and a replicator are followed by a process, indented two spaces. The replicator appears to the right of the keyword **PAR**. The replicator specifies a name for the index. The value of the index for the first replication is the value of the base expression, and the number of times the process is replicated is the value of the count expression.

The index may be used in expressions but cannot be assigned to by an input or assignment. A negative value count expression is *invalid* (see appendix E, page 78 for an explanation of how *invalid processes* behave). If the value of the count expression is zero, the parallel replication behaves like the primitive process **SKIP** (page 7). The base and count expressions of a replicated **PAR** must be constant values.

The index has a value of *type* **INT**. The data type of the base and the count expressions must also be of type **INT**. Data types (page 23) are explained later in the manual.

2.6   Alternation

An alternation combines a number of processes guarded by inputs. The alternation performs the process associated with a guard which is ready. Consider the following example:

```
ALT
  left   ? packet
    stream ! packet
  right ? packet
    stream ! packet
```

The effect of this example is to merge the input from the two channels named **left** and **right**, on to the channel **stream**. The alternation (illustrated in figure 2.3) receives an input from either channel **left** or channel **right**. A ready input is selected, and the associated process is performed. Consider this example in detail. If the channel **left** is ready, and the channel right is not ready, then the input **left ? packet** is selected. If the channel **right** is ready, and the channel left is not ready, then the input **right ? packet** is selected. If neither channel is ready then the alternation waits until an input becomes ready. If both inputs are ready, only one of the inputs and its associated process are performed.

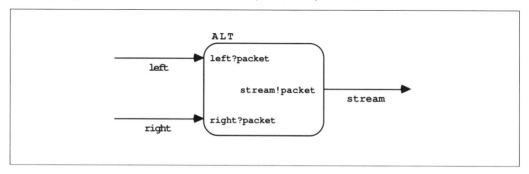

Figure 2.3 Merging the flow of data

A boolean expression may be included in an alternation to selectively exclude inputs from being considered ready, as shown in the following example:

```
ALT
  left.enabled & left   ? packet
    stream ! packet
  right ? packet
    stream ! packet
```

This alternation places the *boolean variable* (page 26) **left.enabled** before the second input.   If **left.enabled** is true, the input is included for consideration by the alternation. If **left.enabled** is false, the input is excluded. To clarify this behaviour, consider the following example:

```
--   Regulator:
--      regulate flow of work into a networked farm
SEQ
  idle := processors
  WHILE running
    ALT
      from.workers ? result
        SEQ
          from.farm ! result
          idle := idle + 1
      (idle >= 1) & to.farm ? packet
        SEQ
          to.workers ! packet
          idle := idle - 1
```

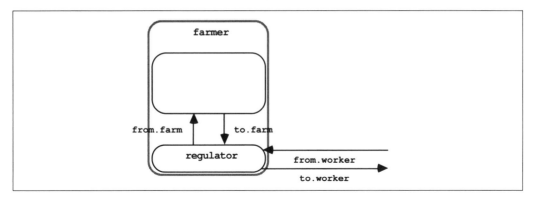

Figure 2.4 Regulating the flow of data

This is an example (part of the farmer process first illustrated in figure 2.2 and fully illustrated in figure 2.4) of a process which regulates the flow of work into a processor *farm*. A processor farm can be thought of as a number of machines (*worker processes*), microcomputers perhaps, each able to perform some task and output a result. The above example controls the amount of work (as packets of data) given to a farm which consists of a network of worker processes. Work may be received by the input **to.farm ? packet**, and is only considered if a member of the farm is idle (i.e. **(idle >= 1)**). As a packet of work is sent to the farm, the counter **idle** is decremented to indicate the number of worker processes which are idle. The worker processes are sent work on the channel **to.workers** (see figure 2.2), and the variable **idle** is decremented to keep a count of the idle machines in the farm. If a worker is busy, the work packet is passed on until a non-busy worker is found.

The syntax for alternation is:

alternation	=	**ALT**
		{ *alternative* }
alternative	=	*guarded.alternative* | *alternation*
guarded.alternative	=	*guard*
		process
guard	=	*input*
	|	*boolean* **&** *input*
	|	*boolean* **&** **SKIP**

The keyword **ALT** is followed by zero or more *alternatives*, indented two spaces. An alternative is either a *guarded* alternative or another alternation. A guarded alternative is an input, or a boolean expression to the left of an ampersand (**&**) with an input or **SKIP** on the right. **SKIP** can take the place of an input in a guard which includes a boolean expression, as shown in the following example:

```
ALT
  in ? data
    out ! data
  monday & SKIP
    out ! no.data
```

If the boolean **monday** is true then **SKIP** is treated as though it where a ready input, and may be selected immediately. If the input **in ? data** is also ready, only one of the processes is performed, which process will be performed is undefined.

Alternation with priority selection is explained in appendix A.2.1, page 72. *Delayed inputs* explained on page 38 will delay before they become ready, and may be used in guards wherever an input may be used.

Inputs (page 6) and **SKIP** (page 7) are discussed in chapter 1. Expressions (page 43) are discussed later in the manual. Details of boolean expressions are given on page 48.

2.6.1   Replicated alternation

An alternation can be replicated in the same way as sequences, conditionals and parallels described earlier in the manual. A replicated alternation constructs a number of similar alternatives. Consider the following example:

```
ALT
    ALT i = 0 FOR number.of.workers
        free.worker[i] & to.farm ? packet
            SEQ
                to.worker[i] ! packet
                free.worker[i] := FALSE

    ALT i = 0 FOR number.of.workers
        from.worker[i] ? result
            SEQ
                from.farm ! result
                free.worker[i] := TRUE
```

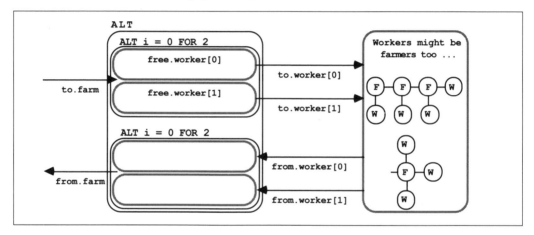

Figure 2.5 A tree structured farm of parallel processes

This example presents an alternate version of the process **farmer** discussed in the previous section and is illustrated in figure 2.5. This version also regulates the flow of work into the farm, but does so by maintaining an array of booleans (**free.worker**) which indicate when a worker is busy. This version of the farmer process is most suitable where several worker processes in the farm are able to input directly from the process. Work packets are input on the channel **to.farm** and distributed to an array of worker processes. The completed result is returned to the farmer process via the channel **from.worker**. Consider first the upper half of this alternation. Each alternative is guarded by a boolean **free.worker[i]** (which has the value true if the worker process is idle), and an input **to.farm ? packet** which inputs packets of work. A selected component of this replication will, after completing the input of a packet, perform the output **to.worker[i] ! packet** (i.e. pass work to an idle worker process), and then set the boolean **free.worker[i]** to false, indicating the worker is no longer idle.

Now consider the lower half of this example, which handles the results returning from worker processes. Each component of the replication is guarded by an input **from.worker[i] ? result** which receives results from a worker process. A selected component of this replication will, after completing the input from the worker process, perform the output **from.farm ! result** (i.e. pass the result back to the process which sent the work), and reset the boolean **free.worker** to true to indicate the worker is now idle.

A number of these farmer processes in parallel can form a tree of worker processes (see figure 2.5), enabling large and effective farms to be built.

If **number.of.workers** has the value 2, the example has the same effect as:

```
ALT
  ALT
    free.worker[0] & to.farm ? packet
      SEQ
        to.worker[0] ! packet
        free.worker[0] := FALSE
    free.worker[1] & to.farm ? packet
      SEQ
        to.worker[1] ! packet
        free.worker[1] := FALSE

  ALT
    from.worker[0] ? result
      SEQ
        from.farm ! result
        free.worker[0] := TRUE
    from.worker[1] ? result
      SEQ
        from.farm ! result
        free.worker[1] := TRUE
```

As for the earlier descriptions of replication, the value of the index for the first replication is the value of the base expression, and the number of replications is the value of the count expression. The syntax for the replicated alternation is:

alternation	=	**ALT** *replicator*
		alternative
replicator	=	*name* = *base* **FOR** *count*
base	=	*expression*
count	=	*expression*

The keyword **ALT** and a replicator are followed by an alternative which is indented two spaces. The replicator appears to the right of the keyword **ALT**. The replicator specifies a name for the index.

The index may be used in expressions but cannot be assigned to by an input or assignment. A negative value count expression is *invalid*. See appendix E, page 78 for an explanation of how *invalid processes* behave. If the value of the count expression is zero, the replicated alternation behaves like the primitive process **STOP** (page 7).

The index has a value of *data type* **INT**. The data type of the base and the count expressions must also be an integer of type **INT**. Data types (page 23) are explained later in the the manual.

3 Data types

occam programs act upon *variables*, *channels* and *timers*. A variable has a value, and may be assigned a value in an *assignment* or *input*. Channels communicate values. Timers produce a value which represents the time.

This chapter describes the *data type* of values, also literal representations of known values, and the declaration of variables.

Channels are discussed on page 29 and timers are discussed on page 37.

3.1 Data types

Values are classified by their *data type*. A data type determines the set of values that may be taken by objects of that type.

These are the primitive data types available in occam:

BOOL	Boolean values true and false.
BYTE	Integer values from 0 to 255.
INT	Signed integer values represented in twos complement form using the word size most efficiently provided by the implementation.
INT16	Signed integer values in the range -32768 to 32767, represented in twos complement form using 16 bits.
INT32	Signed integer values in the range -2^{31} to $(2^{31} - 1)$, represented in twos complement form using 32 bits.
INT64	Signed integer values in the range -2^{63} to $(2^{63} - 1)$, represented in twos complement form using 64 bits.
REAL32	Floating point numbers stored using a sign bit, 8 bit exponent and 23 bit fraction in ANSI/IEEE Standard 754-1985 representation. The value is positive if the sign bit is 0, negative if the sign bit is 1. The magnitude of the value is: $$\begin{array}{ll} (2^{(exponent-127)}) * 1.fraction & \text{if } 0 < exponent \text{ and } exponent < 255 \\ (2^{-126}) * 0.fraction & \text{if } exponent = 0 \text{ and } fraction \neq 0 \\ 0 & \text{if } exponent = 0 \text{ and } fraction = 0 \end{array}$$
REAL64	Floating point numbers stored using a sign bit, 11 bit exponent and 52 bit fraction in ANSI/IEEE Standard 754-1985 representation. The value is positive if the sign bit is 0, negative if the sign bit is 1. The magnitude of the value is: $$\begin{array}{ll} (2^{(exponent-1023)}) * 1.fraction & \text{if } 0 < exponent \text{ and } exponent < 2047 \\ (2^{-1022}) * 0.fraction & \text{if } exponent = 0 \text{ and } fraction \neq 0 \\ 0 & \text{if } exponent = 0 \text{ and } fraction = 0 \end{array}$$

As the above list shows, all signed integer values are represented in twos complement form using the number of bits indicated by the type. All real values are represented according to the representation specified by the ANSI/IEEE standard 754-1985, for binary floating-point arithmetic.

Objects which have values in occam have one of the following forms:

Literals	Textual representation of known values
Constants	Symbolic names which have a constant value
Variables	Symbolic names which have a value, and may be assigned to by input or assignment
Index	Replication index value

A literal is a known value (**1**, **2**, **'H'**, **"Hello"**, etc..). A variable has a value of a specified type, and may be assigned a new value by an input or assignment. Names with a constant value are specified by an *abbreviation* (page 57). *Expressions* (page 43) and *functions* (page 65) also have a data type and value. The name specified as the index of a replication has a different value for each component of the replication.

The syntax of primitive data types is:

```
primitive.type   =     BOOL
                 |     BYTE
                 |     INT
                 |     INT16
                 |     INT32
                 |     INT64
                 |     REAL32
                 |     REAL64
```

Rounding of real values

An accepted limitation in the use of floating point representations of real values is that only a finite set of all possible real values can be represented, thus any real value will be rounded to produce a result which is the nearest value that can be represented by the type. For example, where the type is **REAL32**, the next representable value after 1.0 is the value 1.00000019209 (to the nearest 11 digits past the decimal point), any value lying between 1.0 and this value cannot be exactly represented using the representation of type **REAL32**. Thus, values which do lie between 1.0 and 1.00000019209 which are of type **REAL32** must be *rounded* to one of these values.

The rounding of real numbers occurs in arithmetic expression evaluation (page 43), in explicit *type conversions* (page 49), and also when literals are converted to the IEEE representation. An explanation of the IEEE rounding modes, is given in the appendix (page 79).

3.1.1   Arrays

The previous section describes primitive types. Non-primitive data types are *array types*. Arrays and their declaration are described in detail in chapter 6 on page 39. Arrays are briefly described here for completeness, as an understanding of them is necessary in the following chapter which describes channel protocols. An array has a number of components of the same primitive type. An example of an array type is:

```
[5]INT
```

Arrays of this type have components each of type **INT**. The components are numbered 0, 1, 2, 3, 4. Arrays may have several dimensions. The following example is an array type with two dimensions:

```
[4][5]INT
```

An array of this type has four components each of type **[5]INT**. Array types with any number of dimensions may be constructed. Here are some further examples of array types:

[n]BYTE	byte arrays with **n** components
[3][3][3]REAL32	arrays of real numbers, with three dimensions
[50]BOOL	arrays with boolean components.

The syntax for array types is:

```
array.type   =     [ expression] type
```

The syntax for array types shows that any type can be preceded by a value (of type **INT**) in square brackets, that value specifying the number of components of the type. Primitive and non-primitive types are collectively called *types* (types include channels and timers, as shown later). The above syntax is recursive, and this allows it to cater for multidimensional arrays, as illustrated in the examples above.

3.2   Literals

A literal is a textual representation of a known value, and has a data type. For example, the following are all valid literals:

42	an integer literal in decimal
#2A	an integer literal in hexadecimal
'T'	a byte literal
"zen"	a string literal
TRUE	a boolean literal

A number (e.g. **42**) representing a decimal value, or a hexadecimal value introduced by the hash symbol (**#**), is an integer of type **INT**. A character enclosed within a pair of quotation marks (e.g. **'z'**) has a value of type **BYTE**. A string is an array of bytes, thus the string **"zen"** is an array of type **[3]BYTE**.

Literal values of other types are expressed by stating the type explicitly, for example:

42(BYTE)	a byte value
'T'(INT)	an integer value
42(INT64)	an integer value with 64 bit representation
42.0(REAL32)	a 32 bit floating point value
386.54(REAL64)	a 64 bit floating point value
587.0E-20(REAL64)	a 64 bit floating point value
+1.0E+123(REAL64)	a 64 bit floating point value
16777217.0(REAL32)	a 32 bit floating point value

The type of all real number literals must be stated explicitly in parentheses after the real number. A literal of type **REAL32** or **REAL64** will be rounded (page 24) when the value is converted into the representation of the type. The effect of this rounding can be seen particularly in the last example shown here. The value 16777216.0 is 2^{24} and can be represented precisely in the representation of 32 bit real numbers with a fraction of 23 bits. However, the value 16777217.0 is (2^{24} + 1) and cannot be represented precisely in this representation, and will round to the value 16777216.0. The nearest unique value of a conversion of a literal of type **REAL32** can be determined from the first 9 significant digits, and from the first 17 significant digits of a literal of type **REAL64**. The routines which perform these conversions will use all the digits given in a literal, but further digits will have no affect on the value, for example:

54321765439.54(REAL32)	has a nearest representable value of 54321766400.0
54321765400.00(REAL32)	also has a nearest representable value of 54321766400.0

An explanation of the IEEE rounding is given in the appendix (page 79).

The syntax for literals is:

```
literal      =        integer
             |        byte
             |        integer (type)
             |        byte (type)
             |        real (type)
             |        string
             |        TRUE | FALSE
integer      =        digits | #hex.digits
byte         =        ' character'
real         =        digits . digits | digits . digits Eexponent
exponent     =        +digits | -digits
digit        =        0 | 1 | 2 | 3 | 4 | 5 | 6 | 7 | 8 | 9
hex.digit    =        digit | A | B | C | D | E | F
```

All characters are coded according to their ASCII code. The character **A**, for example, has a value 65, and so on. A table of the ASCII character set is given in the appendix (appendix I, page 92). A character enclosed in a pair of quotes (e.g. **'T'**) is a byte value, unless explicitly stated otherwise by placing a type in parentheses to the right of the enclosing quotes.

Strings are a sequence of characters enclosed by double quotes (e.g. **"zen"**). The type of a string is a table of type **BYTE**. Each component of the table is the ASCII value of the corresponding character in the string. Special character sequences allow control values such as Tabulation and Carriage Return values to be included in strings. Full details of the occam character set and special characters are given in the appendix (page 92).

A string may be broken over several lines by terminating broken lines with an asterisk, and starting the continuation on the following line with another asterisk. The indentation of the continuation should be no less than the current indentation, as illustrated in the following example:

```
occam := "Beware the jabberwock my son, the jaws that bite, the*
         * claws that catch, beware the jubjub bird, and shun the*
         * frumious bandersnatch."
```

The literals **TRUE** and **FALSE** represent the boolean values true and false respectively.

3.3   Variables

The declaration of a variable declares the data type and name of the variable. Consider the following example:

```
INT n :
```

This declaration declares an integer variable of type **INT**, and identifies the variable with the name **n**. The variable is not initialised, and therefore the value of the variable is unspecified until assigned to by an input or assignment. An assignment or input to a variable is valid only if the value to be assigned is the same data type as the variable. Here is a sequence of variable declarations:

```
BOOL    flag :
BYTE    char :
INT64   big :
REAL32  x  :
```

The syntax for a declaration is :

```
declaration   =      type {1 , name } :
```

This syntax applies also to the declaration of channels (page 29) and timers (page 37). A variable declaration consists of the data type, and a name to identify the variable. The declaration appears on a single line, and is terminated by a colon. Where a number of variables of the same type need to be declared, occam permits a single declaration for several names, as shown in the following example:

```
REAL64 a, b, c :
```

The type of the declaration is determined, and then the declarations are performed. This declaration is equivalent to the following sequence of declarations:

```
REAL64 a :
REAL64 b :
REAL64 c :
```

The variable names specified in a multiple declaration are separated by commas. A line break is permitted after a comma. Here are a few more multiple declarations:

```
BOOL flag, switch :
INT16 i, j, k :
REAL64 x, y :
INT64 chains,
      more.chains :
```

Details of arrays and their declaration are given on page 39.

4 Channels

occam programs act upon *variables*, *channels* and *timers*. A variable has a value, and may be assigned a value in an *assignment* or *input*. Channels communicate values. Timers produce a value which represents the time.

This chapter describes channels, the declaration of channels, and the specification of the format and data type of communication.

Variables (page 23) and timers (page 37) are discussed elsewhere in the manual.

Channels provide unbuffered, unidirectional point-to-point communication of values between two concurrent processes. The format and type of values passed on a channel is specified by the channel *protocol*. The name and protocol of a channel are specified in a channel declaration.

4.1   Channel type

The type of a channel is:

 CHAN **OF** *protocol*

As the syntax shows, channels are a primitive type, just like data types and timers:

 primitive.type =   **CHAN** **OF** *protocol*

4.2   Declaring a channel

A channel is declared in just the same way as variables are declared. Consider the following example:

        CHAN OF BYTE screen :

This declaration declares a channel named **screen** with a protocol of type **BYTE**. The protocol in this example specifies that each communication on this channel must be a value of type **BYTE**. An output on this channel could be:

        screen ! 'H'

Several channels with the same protocol can be declared together, for example:

        CHAN OF BYTE screen, keyboard :

The type of the declarations is determined, and then the declarations are made.

Arrays are described in chapter 6 which starts on page 39.

4.3   Channel protocol

A channel communicates values between two concurrent processes. The format and data type of these values is specified by the channel protocol. The channel protocol is specified when the channel is declared. Each input and output must be compatible with the protocol of the channel used. Channel protocols enable the compiler to check the usage of channels.

4.3.1   Simple protocols

The simplest protocols consist of a primitive data type, or an array data type. An example of a channel with a byte protocol has already been given. A protocol with an array type can be declared in the same way, for example:

```
CHAN OF [36]BYTE message :
```

This declaration declares a channel with a byte array protocol which is identified by the name **message**. The protocol of this channel specifies that the channel is able to pass byte arrays with **36** components. For example, consider this output:

```
message ! "The vorpal blade went snicker-snack."
```

It is often desirable to have a channel that will pass arrays of values, where the number of components in the array is not known until the output occurs. A special protocol, called a *counted array* protocol, enables this kind of array communication by passing a length first, and then that number of components from the array. A declaration for such a channel looks like this:

```
CHAN OF INT::[]BYTE message :
```

This declaration declares a channel which passes an integer value first, then that number of components from the array. An output on this channel will look like this:

```
message ! 16::"The vorpal blade went snicker-snack."
```

This has the effect of outputting the string **"The vorpal blade"**; the first **16** characters of the array. The associated input could look like this:

```
message ? len::buffer
```

This input will first receive an integer value (**16** in this example) which is assigned to the variable **len**, then that number of components are input and assigned to the first components of the array **buffer**. The input is invalid if the number of components in **buffer** is less than **len**.

All the above protocols are called *simple protocols*, their syntax is:

```
simple.protocol    =        type
                   |        primitive.type :: [] type
input              =        channel ? input.item
input.item         =        variable
                   |        variable :: variable
output             =        channel ! output.item
output.item        =        expression
                   |        expression :: expression
protocol           =        simple.protocol
```

This syntax has extended the syntax for *input* and *output* (see page 6). A simple protocol is either a data type or a counted array as described above, and is specified by the data type of the count (which may be either an integer or byte), followed by a double colon, square brackets (:: []), and the specifier indicating the type of the components.

4.3.2   Naming a protocol

A protocol can be given a name in a *protocol definition*, as shown in the following example:

        PROTOCOL CHAR IS BYTE :

A channel can now be declared with the protocol **CHAR**, for example:

        CHAN OF CHAR screen :

A protocol definition must be used if more complex protocols, like the *sequential protocol* described in the following section are required. The syntax for protocol definition is:

definition	=	**PROTOCOL** *name* **IS** *simple.protocol* :
	|	**PROTOCOL** *name* **IS** *sequential.protocol* :
protocol	=	*name*

A protocol definition defines a name for the simple protocol or sequential protocol (described in the following section) which appears to the right of the keyword **IS**. A protocol definition appears on a single line, and is terminated by a colon. The line may be broken after the keyword **IS** or after a semi-colon in a sequential protocol. It is recommended that the names of protocols be uppercase.

4.3.3   Sequential protocol

Simple protocols have been discussed earlier. Sequential protocols specify a protocol for communication which consists of a sequence of simple protocols. Consider the following example:

        PROTOCOL COMPLEX IS REAL64; REAL64 :

Channels declared with this protocol (**CHAN OF COMPLEX**) pass pairs of values. An input or output on a channel with sequential protocol is a sequence of distinct inputs or outputs. An input on a channel with the above protocol **complex** is shown below:

        items ? real.part; imaginary.part

Each value is input in sequence and assigned to each variable in turn. Here are some more examples of sequential protocol definitions:

```
PROTOCOL DIR.ENTRY IS INT16; [14]BYTE :
PROTOCOL INODE IS INT16;INT16;INT32;INT32;INT16;[7]INT16;INT16;INT16 :
PROTOCOL RECORD IS INT16::[]BYTE :
```

Declarations of channels with these protocols would look like this:

        CHAN OF DIR.ENTRY directory :
        CHAN OF INODE   sys :
        CHAN OF RECORD blocks :

The syntax for sequential protocol is:

sequential.protocol	=	{$_1$; *simple.protocol* }
input	=	*channel* ? {$_1$; *input.item* }
output	=	*channel* ! {$_1$; *output.item* }

A sequential protocol is one or more simple protocols separated by semi-colons. The communication on a channel with a sequential protocol is valid provided the type of each item input or output is compatible with the corresponding component of the protocol.

4.3.4   Variant protocol

It is often convenient to use a single channel to communicate messages with different formats. A *variant protocol* specifies a number of possible formats for communication on a single channel. Consider the following example:

```
PROTOCOL FILES
  CASE
    request;   BYTE
    filename;  [14]BYTE
    word;      INT16
    record;    INT32; INT16::[]BYTE
    error;     INT16; BYTE::[]BYTE
    halt
  :
```

This example defines a variant protocol named **FILES**. **CASE** combines a number of *tags*, each of which may identify a sequential protocol. The variant protocol defined here has six variants. It is important to note that this protocol definition defines seven new names, the name of the protocol **FILES**, and the names of the six tags, **request**, **filename**, **word**, **record**, **error**, **halt**. A channel declared with this protocol would look like this:

```
CHAN OF FILES to.dfs :
```

A communication on this channel first sends a tag to inform the receiving process of the format for the rest of the communication. So, for example

```
to.dfs ! request; get.record
```

first sends the tag **request** followed by a **BYTE** value (**get.record**). Consider the output:

```
to.dfs ! halt
```

This output sends only the tag **halt** and according to the above variant protocol definition requires no further output.

The syntax for a variant protocol and the associated output is:

definition	=	**PROTOCOL** *name*
		CASE
		{ *tagged.protocol* }
		:
tagged.protocol	=	*tag*
	|	*tag ; sequential.protocol*
tag	=	*name*
output	=	*channel* ! *tag*
	|	*channel* ! *tag ; {$_1$; output.item }*

In a definition of a variant protocol the name which identifies the protocol appears to the right of the keyword **PROTOCOL**, this is followed at an indentation of two spaces by the keyword **CASE**, which in turn is followed at a further indentation of two spaces by a number of tagged protocols. The definition of a variant protocol is terminated by a colon, which appears on a line by itself, at the same level of indentation as the **P** of the keyword **PROTOCOL**. A tagged protocol is either a tag by itself or a tag followed by a semi-colon, and sequential protocol. Tags are a name like any other name, they must be distinct and are specified (that is, brought into existence) by the variant protocol definition.

An output on a channel of variant protocol is a tag by itself or a tag followed by a number of output items separated by semi-colons. The output is valid only if the tag and the associated output items are compatible with one of the tagged protocols specified in the definition.

Input on a channel with variant protocol

So far only output on a channel with variant protocol has been shown. A special form of input is required (called *case input*) to provide for input on channels with a variant protocol. The previous example is suggestive of a *conversation* with a *disc filing system*, and is a reminder that channels are unidirectional. So, for a user process to "listen to" the other side of this conversation, another channel must be declared, as shown below:

```
CHAN OF FILES from.dfs :
```

This example declares another channel with the protocol **FILES**. The process which outputs **request; get.record**, might reasonably expect to receive a reply on a channel with this protocol. Consider a more complete example of this conversation:

```
SEQ
  to.dfs ! request; get.record
  from.dfs ? CASE
    record; rnumber; rlen::buffer
      ... do whatever
    error;  enumber; elen::buffer
      ... handle error
```

Illustrated in the above example is a case input on the channel **from.dfs**. This accepts a variant input with either the tag **record** or the tag **error**, any other tag would be invalid and the input would behave like the primitive process **STOP**.

A special form of case input simply receives a tag from the channel named on the left of the case input symbol (**? CASE**), and then compares the tag for equality with the tag of the tagged list which appears to the right of the symbol. A tag is input, then if the tags match the process next inputs the remainder of the tagged list, if the tags do not match the process next behaves like the primitive process **STOP**, for example:

```
from.dfs ? CASE filename; name.buffer
```

This process inputs a tag, if the tag is **filename** the input is completed, and a value assigned to the variable **name.buffer**. Otherwise, no further input is performed, and the input behaves like the primitive process **STOP** (page 7). A case input is valid only if the tagged lists are compatible with one of the tagged protocols specified in the definition.

Consider the following:

```
PROTOCOL COMMS
  CASE
    packet;INT::[]BYTE
    sync
:
CHAN OF COMMS route :
PAR
  SEQ
    route ! packet; 11::"Hello world"
    R ()
  SEQ
    route ? CASE sync
    S ()
```

In this example the input **route ? CASE sync** will behave like the primitive process **STOP** as the tags do not match. The associated output will also behave like **STOP**, for although the output of the tag **packet** succeeds, the output **11::"Hello world"** does not. In this example the procedures **R ()** and **S ()** will not be performed. Also consider the following:

```
PAR
  SEQ
    route ! sync
    P ()
  SEQ
    route ? CASE packet; length::message
    Q ()
```

Each communication of sequential protocol, or of a tagged sequential protocol is in fact a sequence of separate communications. So, in the above example, the input **route ? CASE packet; length::message** will behave like the primitive process **STOP** because the tags do not match. However, the associated output **route ! sync** will succeed as the output of the tag has completed, and the variant requires no further output. Thus, the *procedure* (page 61) **P ()** will be performed, and the procedure **Q ()** will not be performed. The syntax for case input is:

case.input	=	*channel* ? **CASE**
		{ *variant* }
variant	=	*tagged.list*
		process
	|	*specification*
		variant
tagged.list	=	*tag*
	|	*tag ;* {$_1$ *; input.item* }
process	=	*case.input*
input	=	*channel* ? **CASE** *tagged.list*

A case input receives a tag from the channel named on the left of the case input symbol (**? CASE**), and then the tag is used to select one of the variants. These appear on the following lines, indented by two spaces. A tag is input, then if a variant with that tag is present the process next inputs the remainder of the tagged list, and an associated process, indented a further two spaces, is performed. If no variant with that tag is found the process next behaves like the primitive process **STOP**.

A case input may consist of a tagged list only, as shown in the earlier examples.

Variants in alternatives

Case inputs may also be used as an input in an alternation (chapter 2, page 18). Consider the following example:

```
ALT
  from.dfs ? CASE
    request; query
      ... do query
    error; enumber; elen::buffer
      ... handle dfs error
    record; rnumber; rlen::buffer
      ... accept record

  from.network ? CASE
    request; query
      ... do query
    error; enumber; elen::buffer
      ... handle network error
    record; rnumber; rlen::buffer
      ... accept record
```

This alternation accepts input from either of the two channels (**from.dfs** and **from.network**). These inputs are explained in the previous section. This alternation could have included a mix of case inputs, and the alternatives described on page 18. The syntax for case inputs in an alternative is:

alternative   =   *channel* ? **CASE**
                           { *variant* }
                 | *boolean* & *channel* ? **CASE**
                           { *variant* }

A case input as an alternative is either a case input with variants as described in the earlier syntax, or such a case input preceded by a boolean guard and an ampersand (**&**) to the left of the channel name. The case input is not considered by the alternation if the boolean guard is false.

4.3.5   Anarchic protocol

In some situations it may be necessary to specify a channel protocol where the format of the protocol for some reason cannot be defined. Such situations are rare, and are likely to occur only when communicating with an external device such as a printer, terminal or other device controller. Such a device can be considered an *alien process* where the protocol for communication with that process is dictated by the nature of the device. A special protocol exists which allows the input and output of any format without checking. The protocol is specified by the keyword **ANY**, as illustrated in the following example:

>   **CHAN OF ANY printer :**

A channel with this protocol can only input or output values of data type. The effect of an output on a channel with the **ANY** protocol is that the value is mapped down into its constituent bytes, and output as an array of bytes. An input on a channel with the **ANY** protocol inputs the array of bytes and converts (by retyping conversion, see page 77) the value to the type of the receiving variable.

5 Timers

occam programs act upon *variables*, *channels* and *timers*. A variable has a value, and may be assigned a value in an *assignment* or *input*. Channels communicate values. Timers produce a value which represents the time.

This chapter describes timers, the declaration of timers, and access to them.

Channels are discussed on page 29 and variables are discussed on page 23.

A timer provides a clock which can be accessed by any number of concurrent processes.

5.1   Timer type

The type of a timer is:

    TIMER

Timers are a primitive type, just like channels and data types. Here is the syntax:

 primitive.type   =   **TIMER**

5.2   Declaring a timer

A timer is declared in a manner similar to channels and variables. Consider the following example:

    TIMER clock :

This declaration declares a timer which is identified by the name **clock**. Several timers may be declared together, for example:

    TIMER clockA, clockB :

The type of the declarations are determined, and then the declarations are made. *Arrays* of timers are discussed later in the manual (page 40).

A value input from a timer provides an integer value of type **INT** representing the time. The value is derived from a clock, which changes by an increment at regular intervals. The value of the clock is. cyclic (i.e. when the value reaches the most positive integer value, an increment results in the most negative integer value). The special operator **AFTER** can be used to compare times even though the value may have crossed from most positive to most negative, just as one o'clock *pm* may be considered later than eleven o'clock *am*. If **t1** and **t2** are successive inputs from the same timer, then the expression **t1 AFTER t2** is true if **t1** is later than **t2**. This behaviour is only sensible if the second value (**t2**) is input within one cycle of the timer. **AFTER** is also explained in the chapter on expressions (page 43).

The rate at which a timer is incremented is implementation dependent.

5.3   Timer input

Timers are accessed by special forms of *input* called *timer inputs*, which are similar to channel inputs, for example:

```
clock ? t
```

This example inputs a value from the timer `clock` and assigns the value to the variable `t`. Unlike channels, inputs from the same timer may appear in any number of components of a parallel.

Another special input (called a *delayed input*) specifies a time, after which the input terminates, for example:

```
clock ? AFTER t
```

This input waits until the value of the timer `clock` is later than the value of `t`. In other words, if `c` is the value of the timer `clock`, then the input will wait until `(c AFTER t)` is true. The value of `t` is unchanged.

More usefully perhaps, a delay can be caused by this sequence:

```
SEQ
    clock ? now
    clock ? AFTER now PLUS delay
```

This sequence inputs a value representing the current time and assigns it to the variable **now**. The following delayed input waits until the value input from `clock` is later than the value of **now PLUS delay**. **PLUS** (page 46) is a *modulo operator*.

The syntax for timer inputs is:

input	=	*timer input*
	|	*delayed input*
timer input	=	*timer* ? *variable*
delayed input	=	*timer* ? **AFTER** *expression*

A timer input receives a value from the timer named on the left of the input symbol (**?**), and assigns that value to the variable named on the right of the symbol. A delayed input waits until the value of the timer named on the left of the input symbol (**?**) is later than the value of the expression on the right of the keyword **AFTER**.

6 Arrays and elements

Previous chapters have described types in occam and the declaration of *variables*, *channels* and *timers*. This chapter describes arrays, and the syntactic components of a program which describe *elements* of these types.

An array has a number of consecutively numbered components of the same primitive type. Elements enable channels, timers, variables or arrays to be selected from arrays. An element is either a name, a *subscripted* name, or a *segment*. An element which is a name identifies a variable or array of variables, a channel or array of channels, a timer or array of timers.

6.1   Data type arrays

Primitive types have already been discussed in some detail. Non-primitive data types are *array types*. An example of an array type is:

```
[5]INT
```

Arrays of this type have components each of type **INT**. The components are numbered 0, 1, 2, 3, 4. The declaration of an array follows the same form as other declarations, for example:

```
[5]INT x :
```

This declaration declares an integer array **x** with five components. Arrays may have further dimensions specified by simply adding the size of the dimension, enclosed in square brackets, to the type. The following is an array type with two dimensions:

```
[4][5]INT
```

An array of this type has four components each of type **[5]INT**. Equally, an array of type **[3][4][5]INT** is an array with three components of type **[4][5]INT**, and so on. In this way, arrays with any number of dimensions may be constructed. The declaration of an array with multiple dimensions is similar to other declarations, as shown in the following example:

```
[4][5]INT x :
```

In theory there is no limit to the number of dimensions an array type may have. In practice however, arrays of data type require memory, and therein lies the limit. Here are some more array types:

`[n]BYTE`	a byte array with **n** components
`[3][3][3]REAL32`	a three dimensional array of real numbers
`[50]BOOL`	an array with boolean components.

The size of each dimension in an array declaration must be specified by a value of type **INT**, and be a value greater than zero. Two arrays of data type are considered to have the same type if they have the same number and type of components. An array may be assigned to by input or assignment. An input or assignment to an array is valid only if the value to be assigned is of the same type as the array. Here are a few more examples of array declarations:

```
[4]BOOL flag :
[5]INT v1, v2 :
[maxlen]BYTE string :
[xsize][ysize]REAL64 matrix :
[3][3][3]INT16 cube :
```

The syntax for array types is:

```
type       =    primitive.type
           |    array.type
array.type =    [ expression] type
```

The syntax for array types shows that any type can be preceded by a value (of type **INT**) in square brackets, that value specifying the number of components of the type. Primitive and non-primitive types are collectively called *types* (types include channels and timers, as shown in the next section). The syntax is defined recursively, and this allows the syntax to cater for multidimensional arrays, as illustrated in the examples above.

The declaration of arrays follows from the syntax for declaration described on page 26. Several arrays of the same type can be declared together, for example:

```
[users]INT id, privilege ,:
```

The type of the declarations are determined, and then the declarations are made. This is especially important in the declaration of arrays. Consider the following rather silly declaration:

```
[forms]INT forms, teachers :
```

This example is therefore equivalent to the following sequence:

```
SEQ
  t := forms
  [t]INT forms :
  [t]INT teachers :
```

6.2   Channel arrays and timer arrays

The previous section has described arrays of data type. Arrays of channels and arrays of timers can be declared in the same way. The following, for example, declares an array of channels:

```
[4]CHAN OF BYTE screens :
```

This declaration declares an array **screens** of four channels. The following declares an array of timers:

```
[4]TIMER clock :
```

This declaration declares an array **clock** of four timers.

Multidimensional arrays of channels and timers are built in the same way as multidimensional arrays of variables, for example:

```
[3][4]TIMER clock.clock :
[5][5]CHAN OF PACKETS node :
```

There is a subtle semantic distinction to be made between an array of data type and arrays of channels and timers. An array of variables is itself a variable (it may be assigned to by assignment or input), however, an array of channels is not itself a channel (that is, only single components of the array may be used in input/output) but a means of referencing a number of distinct channels identified by consecutive subscripts. The same is true for arrays of timers.

Several arrays of the same type can be declared together. Consider the following example:

```
[users]CHAN OF BYTE screen, keyboard :
```

The type of the declarations are determined, and then the declarations are made.

6.3   Elements

Elements have a type. Elements which have a *data type* are variables, and also have a value. Elements of *channel type* are used for *input* and *output* (page 6). Elements of *timer type* are used in a *timer input* or *delayed input* (page 37).

Subscripted names select a component of an array. Suppose `clock`, `user.in` and `data` are declared as follows:

```
[9]TIMER clock :
[12]CHAN OF MESSAGES user.in :
[8][8][8]REAL32 data :
```

Consider these examples:

`clock[0]`	the first component of the array `clock`, of type `TIMER`.
`user.in[9]`	the tenth component of the array `user.in`, of type `CHAN OF MESSAGES`.
`data[0]`	the first component of a dimension of `data`, of type `[8][8]REAL32`.
`data[3][0]`	the first component of another dimension of `data`, of type `[8]REAL32`.

A subscript appears in square brackets after the name of an array. The component selected has one dimension less than its type for each subscript. Subscripts must be an expression of integer type `INT`. A subscript is valid only if the value of the expression is within the bounds of the array, and so a negative value subscript is always invalid. That is, the value of a subscript must be in the range 0 to $(n-1)$, where n is the number of components in the array.

A segment of an array is itself an array. The segment has zero or more components, as shown in the following examples:

`[clock FROM 0 FOR 1]`	the first component of the array `clock`, of type `[1]TIMER`.
`[user.in FROM 9 FOR 1]`	the tenth component of the array `user.in`, of type `[1]CHAN OF MESSAGES`.
`[user.in FROM 9 FOR 3]`	the tenth, eleventh and twelfth components of the array `user.in`, of type `[3]CHAN OF MESSAGES`.
`[data FROM 0 FOR n]`	the first n components of `data`, of type `[n][8][8]REAL32`.
`[data FROM n FOR 6]`	six components of the array `data` from n, of type `[6][8][8]REAL32`.
`[data FROM 1 FOR 0]`	an "empty" segment, compatible with a specifier `[][8][8]REAL32`.

A segment of an array has the same number of dimensions as the array.

The syntax for elements is:

```
element   =      element [ subscript ]
          |      [ element FROM subscript FOR count ]
          |      name
subscript =      expression
```

The syntax is defined recursively, and shows how more complex elements can be built. The simplest subscripted element is a name followed by a single subscript in square brackets to the right of the name. This is itself an element and may also be followed by a subscript in square brackets, and so on, limited by the number of dimensions in the array. A segment begins with a square bracket, followed on the right by an element and the keyword **FROM**. This is followed by a subscript, which must be an integer of type `INT`, indicating the first component of the segment, this in turn is followed by the keyword **FOR** and a count, which is a value of type `INT` which specifies the number of components in the segment. Line breaks are permitted immediately after the keyword **FROM** and the keyword **FOR**. The segment is valid only if the value of the count is not negative, and does not violate the bounds of the array. That is, the value must be in the range 0 to $((subscript + count) - 1)$. Here is another example to consider:

> [[c **FROM** j **FOR** i] **FROM** 0 **FOR** 5]

This complex looking segment selects the first five components of an element which is itself a segment, it is in fact equivalent to [c **FROM** j **FOR** 5] provided $i \geq 5$. Segments may also be subscripted, for example:

> [x **FROM** n **FOR** 8] [3]

The subscript in this example selects component number 3 from the associated segment.

An assignment to a variable selected by a subscript is an assignment to that component of the array, and has no effect on any other component in the array. Consider the following example:

> x[3] := 42

Assignment to a segment of a variable which is an array, is not valid if a component of the expression is also a component of the array to which it is to be assigned. Thus, the following assignment is not valid:

> [x **FROM** 6 **FOR** 6] := [x **FROM** 8 **FOR** 6] -- INVALID!

Both these segments share the component x[8]. The effect of an assignment to an array or a segment of an array, is to assign to each component the value of the corresponding component of the expression.

The combined effect of an input and output on a channel of an array or a segment of an array is equivalent to an assignment from the outputting process to the inputting process. Consider the following example:

> [x **FROM** 0 **FOR** 10] := [y **FROM** 0 **FOR** 10]

This is a valid assignment, and has the same effect as the following:

> **PAR**
>   c ! [y **FROM** 0 **FOR** 10]
>   c ? [x **FROM** 0 **FOR** 10]

Also consider the following assignment of **v1** to **v2**, where both are arrays of type [12] **INT**:

> v1 := v2

This assignment assigns each component of the array **v2** to each respective component of the array **v1**, and has the same effect as the following communication:

> **PAR**
>   c ! v1
>   c ? v2

Assignment is discussed earlier on page 5, input and output are also described earlier on page 6. See the appendix (page 78) to discover how invalid processes behave.

7 Expressions

This chapter is about *expressions*, and describes the range of *operators* provided by occam. The chapter also describes *data type conversions* and *tables*.

An expression is evaluated and produces a result. The result of an expression has a value and a data type. The simplest expressions are literals and variables. More complex expressions are constructed from *operands*, operators and *parentheses*. An operand is either an *element* (page 39) of data type, a literal, a table, or another expression enclosed in parentheses. An operator performs an operation, for example an addition, upon its operand(s). The following are all valid expressions:

5(INT64)	a literal value
x	a variable
6 * 4	multiplication of two literal operands
x * y	multiplication of two variable operands
NOT TRUE	a boolean expression

An expression may itself be an operand in an expression. In this way larger expressions are built, as shown in the following examples:

(1 + 2) - 1	subtract 1 from the result of (1 + 2)
(x * y) * (w * z)	multiply the results of the expressions (x * y) and (w * z)

There is no operator precedence as the hierarchical structure of a large expression is clearly defined by parentheses. With the exception of shift operations, where the number of bits shifted is indicated by a value of type **INT**, the data type of the two operands in a dyadic expression must be of the same type. In an assignment the value of the expression must be of the same data type as the variable to which it is to be assigned. Consider in detail the following example:

    y := (m * x) + c

Each of the elements in this expression (**y**, **m**, **x** and **c**) must be of the same data type. The result of an expression is of the same type as its operand(s). The expression in this example - (m * x) + c - has two operators. The parentheses indicate that the expression (m * x) is an operand of the operator +, and thus must be evaluated before the + operation can be performed.

The syntax for expressions is:

expression	=	*monadic.operator operand*
	|	*operand dyadic.operator operand*
	|	*conversion*
	|	*operand*
operand	=	*element*
	|	*literal*
	|	*table*
	|	(*expression*)

Tables, operators and conversions are detailed in the following sections. Elements (page 39) and literals (page 25) have been explained earlier.

7.1   Tables

A table constructs an array of values from a number of expressions which must yield values of the same data type. The value of each component of the array is the value of the corresponding expression. Consider the following example:

```
[1, 2, 3]
```

This example constructs an array with three components, each of type **INT**. Here are some more examples:

['a', 'b', 'c']	a table of three bytes (equivalent to "abc")
[x, y, z]	a table of three values
[x * y, x + 4]	a table with two component values
[(a * b) + c]	a table with a single component
[6(INT64), 8888(INT64)]	a table of two **INT64** integers

If the variables a, b and c are of type **INT**, then the table [(a * b) + c] is an expression whose type is [1] INT. ['a', 'b', 'c'] is an expression whose type is [3] BYTE, and so on.

The syntax for tables is:

```
table  =     table [ subscript ]
       |     [ {₁ , expression } ]
       |     [ table FROM subscript FOR count ]
```

A table is one or more expressions of the same data type, separated by commas, and enclosed in square brackets. Line breaks are permitted after a comma. The meanings of *subscript* and *count* are given earlier in the description of elements (page 39).

7.2   Operations

An operation evaluates its operand(s) and produces a result. The result of an operation has a value and a data type.

+	addition	~	bitwise not
−	subtraction	>>	shift right
*	multiplication	<<	shift left
/	division	AND	boolean and
REM	remainder	OR	boolean or
\	remainder	NOT	boolean not
PLUS	modulo addition	=	equal
MINUS	modulo subtraction	<>	not equal
TIMES	modulo multiplication	<	less than
MOSTNEG	most negative	>	greater than
MOSTPOS	most positive	<=	less than or equal
/\	bitwise and	>=	greater than or equal
\/	bitwise or	AFTER	later than
><	bitwise exclusive or	SIZE	array size

7.2.1 Arithmetic operators

The arithmetic operators are:

+	addition
−	subtraction
*	multiplication
/	division
REM	remainder

Arithmetic operators perform an arithmetic operation upon operands of the same integer or real data type (not on bytes or booleans), for example:

39 + 3	produces a value of 42
45 − 3	produces a value of 42
6 * 7	produces a value of 42
126 / 3	produces a value of 42
128 **REM** 3	produces a value of 2

The final example in this list may also be written: `128 \ 3`. The symbols **REM** and `\` both signify the remainder operation. Except where the result is zero, the sign of an integer remainder operation is the sign of the dividend regardless of the sign of the divisor. The result of an integer division is rounded toward zero (i.e. truncated), for example:

3 / 2	produces a value of 1
(−3) / 2	produces a value of −1
(−9) / 4	produces a value of −2
(−9) **REM** 4	produces a value of −1

Remainder operations on both integers and reals, obey the following law:

$$((x/y) * y) + (x \, \text{REM} \, y) = x$$

It is possible for the result of a real remainder operation to be negative. If x and y are real values, the result of x **REM** y is $(x - (y * n))$, where n is the result of dividing x and y rounded toward the nearest integer. Applying this to the following example, n is 0.75 rounded to the nearest integer (1.0), leaving : $(1.5 - (2.0 * 1.0) = (-0.5)$:

$$1.5 \, (\text{REAL32}) \quad \text{REM} \quad 2.0 \, (\text{REAL32})$$

The operator − is also a monadic negation operator, which has the effect of negating the value of its operand, for example:

− **x**	has the value (0 − **x**)
− 5	minus 5

The result of an arithmetic operation produces a result of the same data type as the operands. An arithmetic operation is not valid if the resulting value cannot be represented by the same data type as the operands, for example where the result of a multiplication of two large integers produces a value which exceeds the range of the type (arithmetic overflow). Division by zero is also treated as invalid.

Here are some examples of real expressions, in which **x** is a value of **39.0 (REAL32)**, and **y** is a value of **3.0 (REAL32)**:

x + y	produces a value of 42.0 of type **REAL32**
x − y	produces a value of 36.0 of type **REAL32**
x * y	produces a value of 117.0 of type **REAL32**
x / y	produces a value of 13.0 of type **REAL32**
x REM y	produces a value of 0.0 of type **REAL32**

Rounding the results of real operations

The result of a real arithmetic expression (which is considered to be infinitely precise) is rounded to the nearest value which can be represented by the type. That is, the value will be adjusted, if necessary, to fit into the representation of its type. The precision of an operation is that of the type of the operands.

Full details of IEEE rounding modes are given in the appendix (page 79).

7.2.2   Modulo arithmetic operators

The modulo arithmetic operators are:

PLUS	modulo addition
MINUS	modulo subtraction
TIMES	modulo multiplication

The modulo arithmetic operators perform an operation upon operands of the same integer data type (not on reals, bytes or booleans). The operations perform modulo arithmetic (that is, modulo the range of the type) and thus no overflow can take place. For example, adding one to the most positive integer will produce a value equal to the most negative integer (i.e. $(MOSTPOS$ **PLUS** $1) = MOSTNEG$), and subtracting one from the most negative integer will produce a value equal to the most postive integer (i.e. $(MOSTNEG$ **MINUS** $1) = MOSTPOS$). Consider these examples:

`32767(INT16) + 1(INT16)`	causes an arithmetic overflow. **INVALID!**
`32767(INT16) PLUS 1(INT16)`	produces the value −32768.
`(-32768(INT16)) - 1(INT16)`	causes an arithmetic overflow. **INVALID!**
`(-32768(INT16)) MINUS 1(INT16)`	produces the value 32767.
`20000(INT16) * 10(INT16)`	causes an arithmetic overflow. **INVALID!**
`20000(INT16) TIMES 10(INT16)`	produces the value 3392

MINUS is also a valid monadic operator.

7.2.3   MOSTPOS and MOSTNEG (integer range)

The operator **MOSTPOS** produces the most positive value of an integer type. The operator **MOSTNEG** produces the most negative value of an integer type. Consider the following examples:

MOSTNEG INT16	has the value −32768
MOSTPOS INT16	has the value 32767

The syntax for these operators is:

expression   =   **MOSTPOS** *type*
                   | **MOSTNEG** *type*

The keyword (**MOSTPOS** or **MOSTNEG**) appears to the left of a type.

7.2.4 Bit operations

Bitwise operators perform operations on the bit pattern of a value of integer type. The bitwise operators are:

/\	bitwise and
\/	bitwise or
><	bitwise exclusive or
~	bitwise not

Here are some example expressions using the bitwise operators. The results shown are true if the value of **pixel** is **#1010**, and the value of **pattern** is **#FFFF**, and their type is **INT16**:

pixel /\ pattern	produces a result #1010 (INT16)
~ pixel	produces a result #EFEF (INT16)
pixel \/ pattern	produces a result #FFFF (INT16)
pixel >< pattern	produces a result #EFEF (INT16)

The operands of /\, \/ and >< must both be of the same integer type. The following table illustrates how each bit of the result is produced from the corresponding bits in the operand.

1 >< 0 = 1	1 /\ 0 = 0	1 \/ 0 = 1
0 >< 0 = 0	0 /\ 0 = 0	0 \/ 0 = 0
1 >< 1 = 0	1 /\ 1 = 1	1 \/ 1 = 1
0 >< 1 = 1	0 /\ 1 = 0	0 \/ 1 = 1

The bitwise not operator (~) has a single operand which must be an integer type. Each bit of the result is the inverse of the corresponding bit in the operand, as shown in the following table:

~1 = 0
~0 = 1

The result of a bitwise operation is of the same integer type as the operand(s). The keywords **BITAND**, **BITOR** and **BITNOT** are equivalent to /\, \/, ~ respectively, and are included especially for implementations which have a restricted character set.

7.2.5 Shift operations

the shift operators perform a logical shift on the value of an integer type. The shift operators are:

>>	shift right
<<	shift left

The shift operators shift the bit pattern of a value of any integer type by a number of places determined by a count value of type **INT**. For example, if the value of **n** is **#FFFF**, and of type **INT16**:

n << 4	produces a result #FFF0 (INT16)
n >> 4	produces a result #0FFF (INT16)

The result is of the same integer type as **n**. The bits vacated by the shift become zero, the bits shifted out of the pattern are lost. The left shift operator shifts toward the most significant end of the pattern, the right shift operator shifts toward the least significant end of the pattern.

Consider these further examples, where **n** is a value of type **INT32**:

n << 0	produces the value n
n >> 0	produces the value n
n >> 32	produces the value 0
n << 32	produces the value 0

A shift by a negative value, or by a value which exceeds the number of bits in the representation, is invalid.

7.2.6   Boolean operations

The boolean operators combine operands of boolean type, and produce a boolean result. The boolean operators are:

AND	boolean and
OR	boolean or
NOT	boolean not

The following table shows the results for each operation:

false	**AND**	*true*	*= false*	*false*	**OR**	*true*	*= true*	**NOT**	*false*	*= true*
false	**AND**	*false*	*= false*	*false*	**OR**	*false*	*= false*	**NOT**	*true*	*= false*
true	**AND**	*false*	*= false*	*true*	**OR**	*false*	*= true*			
true	**AND**	*true*	*= true*	*true*	**OR**	*true*	*= true*			

The operand to the left of a boolean operator is evaluated, and if the result of the operation can be determined evaluation ceases. This differs from the behaviour of other expressions. Consider the following example:

```
IF
    ((ch >= 'a') AND (ch <= 'z')) OR ((ch >= 'A') AND (ch <= 'Z'))
    ...
    (ch = cr) OR (ch = down) OR (ch = up)
    ...
    ((ch = escape) AND shift)) OR ((ch = escape) AND control))
    ...
```

Note that parentheses may be omitted between expressions containing adjacent **AND** or **OR** operators. The evaluation of the boolean expression ((ch >= 'a') AND (ch <= 'z')) ceases if the expression (ch >= 'a') is false, the evaluation of the expression (ch <= 'z') does not take place. If the result is true, the expression ((ch >= 'A') AND (ch <= 'Z')) to the right of **OR** is not evaluated. The rule is that evaluation of a boolean expression will cease if the operand to the left of **AND** is false, or if the operand to the left of **OR** is true.

7.2.7   Relational operations

The relational operators perform a comparison of their operands, and produce a boolean result. The relational operators are:

=	equal
<>	not equal
<	less than
>	greater than
<=	less than or equal
>=	greater than or equal

Here are examples of relational expressions using = and <>. In these examples the operands, **x** and **y**, can be any primitive data type:

x = y	is true if the value of **x** is equal to the value of **y** the result is false otherwise
x <> y	is true if the value of **x** is not equal to the value of **y** the result is false otherwise

The following are examples using the other relational operators. In these examples the operands, **x** and **y**, can be an integer, byte or real type, but may not be a boolean:

x < y	is true if the value of **x** is less than the value of **y** the result is false otherwise
x > y	is true if the value of **x** is greater than the value of **y** the result is false otherwise
x <= y	is true if the value of **x** is less than or equal to the value of **y** the result is false otherwise
x >= y	is true if the value of **x** is greater than or equal the value of **y** the result is false otherwise

AFTER (later than)

The special modulo operator **AFTER** performs a comparison operation, and returns a boolean result, for example:

$\qquad$ (a AFTER b)

This expression is true if **a** is later in a cyclic sequence than **b**, just as one o'clock *pm* can be considered later than eleven o'clock *am*. The first operand is considered the starting point on a "clock face" of integer values. If the shortest route to the value of the second operator is clockwise, then the value is later than the first operand and the result of the expression is true. If the shortest route to the value of the second operand is anticlockwise, then the value of the second operand is earlier, and the result of the expression is false.

$(a\,\textbf{AFTER}\,b)$ produces the same value as $(a\,\textbf{MINUS}\,b) > 0$.

7.2.8   SIZE (number of components in an array)

The special operator **SIZE** has a single operand of array type, and produces an integer value of type **INT**, equal to the number of components in the array. For example, if **a** is an array of type **[8] INT**, then:

SIZE a	produces the value 8

If **a** is of type **[8] [4] INT**, then:

SIZE a	produces the value 8
SIZE a[1]	produces the value 4

7.3   Data type conversion

With the exception of logical shifts (where the number of bits to shift must be of type **INT**), the types of the operands in an expression must be of the same type. Operands may explicitly have their data type converted. A data type conversion permits a value of a primitive data type (not array types) to be converted to a numerically similar value of another primitive data type. A data type conversion produces the value of its operand as a value of the specified data type, for example:

```
j := (k * 4.5(REAL64)) * (REAL64 n)
```

The value of **n** in this example is converted to a value of type **REAL64**. Note that **4.5(REAL64)** is a literal value of type **REAL64**, whereas **(REAL64 n)** is a data type conversion of the value of **n**.

The syntax for data type conversions is:

```
conversion   =     primitive.type operand
             |     primitive.type ROUND operand
             |     primitive.type TRUNC operand
```

The type must be a primitive data type, and appears to the left of the operand. A data type conversion which includes the keyword **ROUND** as described by the syntax, produces a value rounded to the nearest value of the specified type. Where two values are equally near, the value is rounded toward the nearest even number. A data type conversion which includes the keyword **TRUNC** as described by the syntax, produces a value truncated (rounded toward zero) to a value of the specified type.

A conversion between any of the integer types, and conversions between those types and type **BYTE**, is valid only if the value produced is within the range of the receiving type. Byte and integer values may be converted to boolean values if their value is one or zero. The boolean value is true if the value is one, and false if the value is zero. That is:

`BOOL 1`	evaluates to **TRUE**
`BOOL 0`	evaluates to **FALSE**
`INT TRUE`	evaluates to 1
`INT FALSE`	evaluates to 0

Conversions from integer values to real values, and vice versa, must specify whether the result is to be rounded or truncated. A value of type **REAL32** can be extended to an exact value of type **REAL64**. Values of type **REAL64** can be converted to values of type **REAL32**, providing the value is in the range of the **REAL32** type. The conversion must specify if the value is to be rounded or truncated. Consider these examples, where **n**, and **m** are integers of type **INT64**, and **n** has a value 255 and **m** has a value 3:

`BYTE n`	produces a byte value 255
`REAL32 ROUND n`	produces a **REAL32** value 255.0
`REAL64 TRUNC n`	produces a **REAL64** value 255.0
`REAL64 ROUND(n * m)`	produces a **REAL64** value 765.0
`(REAL64 ROUND n) * (REAL64 ROUND m)`	produces a **REAL64** value 765.0

Conversions may be applied to operands of the same type, but will have no effect. The truncation and rounding of integer types to real types occurs where the integer cannot be exactly represented as a value of the real type. Consider the following example:

```
SEQ
  i := 33554435 (INT32)    -- hex #2000003
  a := REAL32 ROUND i
  b := REAL32 TRUNC i
```

The value in this example has been chosen specifically to illustrate the behaviour of explicitly rounding an integer value which cannot be directly represented in the floating point representation of **REAL32**. The value of **a** after this sequence is 33554436.0, and the value of **b** is 33554432.0. For **b**, the two least significant bits of the integer representation have been lost they had held the value 3. For **a** the value of those bits has been rounded to the next nearest representable value. Further detail of rounding is given in the appendix on page 79.

Conversion of real values to integers has the effect illustrated by the following examples:

`INT32 ROUND 0.75(REAL32)`	produces a value of 1
`INT32 ROUND 0.25(REAL32)`	produces a value of 0
`INT32 TRUNC 0.75(REAL32)`	produces a value of 0
`INT32 TRUNC 0.25(REAL32)`	produces a value of 0

Consider these examples, where **x**, and **y** are type **REAL32**, **x** has a value 3.5, **y** has a value 2.5.:

`INT16 TRUNC y`	produces the value 2, **y** truncated
`INT16 ROUND y`	produces the value 2, **y** rounded (even)
`INT32 ROUND x`	produces the value 4, **x** rounded (even)
`INT16 TRUNC (x / y)`	produces the value 1
`(INT ROUND x) * 10`	produces the value 40
`REAL64 x`	produces the value 3.5

A full explanation of the IEEE rounding modes is given in the appendix (page 79).

8 Scope

Earlier chapters of this manual describe how occam programs are built from *processes* (page 9), and how smaller processes are combined to form larger processes. The manual has also described ways that names may be specified. A name in an occam program denotes one of the following:

Variable	page 26
Channel	page 29
Timer	page 37
Protocol	page 31
Tag	page 32
Abbreviation	page 57
Procedure	page 61
Function	page 65
Replication index	page 9

Associated with each name is a region of the program in which the name is valid, called the *scope*, for example:

```
INT n :                   -- declare variable n
SEQ                        -- scope of n
  n := 0                   --
  WHILE n < 10             --
    n := n + 1             --
```

This example performs a count of ten using the variable **n** which is declared for the sequence. This variable exists only within the associated scope (illustrated by the comments), and has no existence outside that scope. In the following example two unrelated variables are given the same name (**x**), each variable exists independently within its own scope.

```
TIMER t :                                         -- declare timer
PAR                                                -- scope
  REAL32 x :              -- real variable          --
  SEQ                      -- scope                   --
    x := y + 1            --                          --
    ...                    --                          --
                                                      --
  INT x :                -- integer variable          --
  SEQ                      -- scope                     --
    t ? x                 --                          --
    ...                    --                          --
```

The scope of a name is illustrated by the level of program indentation. The scope of a name includes any other specification which may immediately follow at the same level of indentation, and encompasses all greater levels of indentation in the program. The illustrated scope concludes when the level of indentation returns to the same or lesser level, as the following example shows :

```
SEQ
  INT max :              -- specify max
  INT min :                -- scope of max   -- specify min
  SEQ                       --                   -- scope of min
    c ? max; min           --                   --
    IF                      --                   --
      p < max              --                   --
        p := p + 1         --                   --
      p = max              --                   --
        p := min           --                   --
  SEQ
    ...
```

This example increments **p** if it is less than the value specified by **max**. The scope associated with the variable **p** in this example begins at the declaration of **p** earlier in the program. The association of a name with any particular scope is either *local*, that is, it is specified at the start of the scope under consideration, or the name is *free* of local association. That is, the name is specified at an outer level of scope (as for **p** in the above example) which includes the scope under consideration. If a specification is made which uses an existing name then the new meaning supersedes the old meaning for the duration of the scope of the new specification, as illustrated by the following example:

```
INT x  :                                     -- integer variable x
SEQ                                             -- scope
   dm ? x                                       --
   ALT                                          --
      REAL32 x :              -- real x hides integer variable x
      rs ? x                    -- scope
         . . .                  --
      dm ? y                                    --
         . . .                                  --
   . . .                                        --
```

The second declaration of **x** in the above example, has the effect of "hiding" the earlier use of the name **x** for the duration of its scope. All names within a scope in occam are distinct. That is, a name may only have one meaning within any scope.

Names of keywords may not be used in specifications.

The following syntax specifies at which point in a program a declaration, abbreviation, or definition may occur, and the scope associated with each:

process	=	*specification*
		process
choice	=	*specification*
		choice
option	=	*specification*
		option
alternative	=	*specification*
		alternative
variant	=	*specification*
		variant
valof	=	*specification*
		valof
specification	=	*declaration*
		abbreviation
		definition

A specification is a declaration, an abbreviation (page 57) or a definition (e.g. Protocol definition, page 29). A specificiation may appear before a process, choice, option, alternative, variant, or valof (See *functions* page 65). The region of the program in which a specified name is valid includes any other specification that may immediately follow at the same level of indentation, and the corresponding process, choice, option, alternative, variant or valof.

8.1   Names in the scope of parallel constructs

Component processes of a parallel must not violate the rules which govern the use of variables and channels. This section describes the usage rules which are checked by the occam compiler.

Variables which are assigned to by input or assignment in one of the processes of a parallel may not appear in any other process in the parallel. Also, an array can be used in only one component of a parallel if components of the array are selected by a variable subscript, i.e. a subscript which is dependent on a variable, or a replication index with a variable base or count. A variable may appear in an expression in any component of a parallel, provided the variable is not assigned to by input or assignment in any other component in the parallel. Consider the following example:

```
INT mice :                      -- THIS PARALLEL IS INVALID!
PAR
  SEQ
    mice := 42                  -- cannot assign to the same variable
    c ! 42
  c ? mice                      -- in more than one process in a parallel
```

This process is invalid because it assigns to the variable **mice** in the assignment **mice := 42** in one component of the parallel, and also in the input **c ? mice** in a second component. Also consider the following example:

```
PAR                             -- THIS PARALLEL "MAY" BE INVALID!
  c1 ? data[i]
  c2 ? data[j]
```

The validity of this parallel is dependent upon i and j. If the value of either i or j may change, for example if one is a variable or a replicator index with a variable base or count, then the parallel is invalid. If the value of both are constant, the parallel is valid provided i and j select different components of the array **data**. This ensures that no component of an array is misused. An array may be divided between several parallel processes, and components of those disjoint parts may be selected using variable subscripts, provided each part of the array is referenced by an abbreviation discussed in the following chapter.

A check list of the usage rules which apply to parallel processes is given in the appendix on page 75.

9 Abbreviation

This chapter describes occam abbreviations. There are two kinds of abbreviations: abbreviations which specify a name for an *expression* (page 43), and abbreviations which specify a name for an *element* (page 39). The name specified in an abbreviation is an *alias* for the expression or element.

9.1 Abbreviation of expressions

The first kind of abbreviation to consider is the abbreviation of an expression. This kind of abbreviation can be used to specify a name for a constant value. Consider the following example:

```
VAL INT days.in.week IS 7 :
```

This abbreviation specifies the name **days.in.week** for the constant value 7. Here are some more abbreviations for expressions:

`VAL REAL32 y IS (m * x) + c :`	specifies a name for the current value of an expression
`VAL INT n IS m :`	specifies a name for the current value of the element **m**
`VAL []BYTE vowels IS` `['a', 'e', 'i', 'o', 'u'] :`	specifies a name for a table of constant values

The abbreviated expression must be a valid expression, that is, it must not overflow, and all subscripts must be in range. Variables used in an abbreviated expression may not be assigned to by an input or assignment within the *scope* (page 53, the region of a program where a name is valid) of the abbreviation. This ensures that the value of the expression remains constant for the scope of the abbreviation. For example, in the following abbreviation

```
VAL REAL32 y IS (m * x) + c :
```

no assignment or input may be made to **m**, **x**, or **c** within the scope of **y** of this abbreviation. The effect of the abbreviation is the same as each instance of **y** being replaced by the abbreviated expression. Similarly for the following abbreviation of the expression `[screen FROM line FOR length]`

```
VAL []INT scan IS [screen FROM line FOR length] :
```

no assignment or input may be made to **screen**, **line**, or **length**, within the scope of **scan**. The effect of the abbreviation is the same as each instance of **scan** being replaced by the abbreviated expression, thus

```
VAL []INT scan IS [screen FROM line FOR length] :
SEQ
   row := scan
   ...
```

is equivalent to

```
SEQ
   row := [screen FROM line FOR length]
   ...
```

The syntax for abbreviations of expressions is:

abbreviation	=	**VAL** *specifier name* **IS** *expression* :
	|	**VAL** *name* **IS** *expression* :
specifier	=	*primitive.type*
	|	[ ] *specifier*
	|	[*expression*] *specifier*

The abbreviation of a value begins with the keyword **VAL**. An optional specifier, (which specifies the data type of the abbreviation,) appears to the right of **VAL**, followed by the name, and the keyword **IS**. The abbreviated expression appears to the right of the keyword `IS`. Line breaks are permitted after the keyword `IS`. The type of the expression must be of the same data type as the specifier. The specifier can usually be omitted from the abbreviation, as the type can be inferred from the type of the expression. A specifier `[]` *type* simply defines the abbreviation as being an array with components of the specified type.

9.2   Abbreviation of elements

occam abbreviations may also specify a name for an element of any type. A variable, channel, timer, or array that is within the current scope may be given a name in an abbreviation of this kind, for example:

```
INT n IS m :
```

This abbreviation specifies the name `n` as the new name for `m`. Also, consider the following example:

```
CHAN OF INT user IS lines[8]  :
```

This abbreviation specifies the name **user** for a component of the array **lines**. All subscript expressions used in an abbreviation must be valid. The type of the abbreviated element must be the same as the specifier, so in this example, **lines** has to be an array of **CHAN OF INT**. Other components of the array **lines** may be used only in abbreviations within the scope (page 53) of **user**, but they must not include the component **lines[8]**. Here are some more examples of abbreviations:

`x IS y :`	specifies a new name **x** for **y**
`INT c IS a[1]  :`	specifies a name for a component of the array **a**
`[]REAL32 s IS [a FROM 8 FOR n]  :`	specifies a name for a segment of **a**
`TIMER my.time IS clock[me]  :`	specifies a name for an element of an array of timers

An abbreviation simply provides a name to identify an existing element. The name **my.time** in the above example identifies the existing element **clock[me]**. In the scope of the abbreviation, **my.time ? t** is a timer input from the original timer **clock[me]**. A variable used in a subscript to select a component or components of an array may not be assigned to within the *scope* of the abbreviation. For example, no assignment or input can be made to **me** within the scope of **my.time**. As a result the abbreviation always refers to the same variable throughout its scope. This allows various optimisations to be provided, such as evaluating any expression within the abbreviated element only once. The original element **clock[me]** may not be used within the scope of the abbreviation **my.time**. Where the abbreviation is of an element of an array no other reference may be made to any other part of that array, except in a further abbreviation. Consider the following example:

```
[60][72]INT page :
 ...
   first.line IS page[0]   :
   last.line  IS page[59]  :
   SEQ
     first.line := last.line
     last.line  := page[58]            -- This assignment is INVALID!
     ...
     next.to.last.line IS page[58] : -- This abbreviation is valid
     last.line  := next.to.last.line -- and so too, this assignment
     ...
```

Also consider the following example:

```
WHILE i < limit
   this.line IS page[i] :
   next.line IS page[i+1]  :
   SEQ
     this.line := next.line
       ...
     i = i + 1                        -- this assignment is INVALID!
```

The assignment in the above example is invalid as **i** is used to select components of the array **page** in an abbreviation within the scope of the assignment. This is how the above should be written:

```
WHILE i < limit
  SEQ
    this.line IS page[i] :
    next.line IS page[i+1] :
    SEQ
      this.line := next.line
      ...
    i = i + 1
```

It is important to ensure that all the components of an array remain identified by a single name within any given *scope*. Identification of any component of an array by more than one name constitutes an invalid usage of the component, and it is especially important to be aware this of when abbreviating components of an array. Once any component of an array is abbreviated then reference to other components of the array must be made by further abbreviation. Checks are made to ensure that two abbreviations which identify segments from the same array do not overlap. Further discussion on abbreviation is given in the chapter on procedures (page 61).

The syntax for abbreviations of elements is:

abbreviation	=	*specifier name* **IS** *element* :
	|	*name* **IS** *element* :
specifier	=	*primitive.type*
	|	**[]** *specifier*
	|	**[** *expression* **]** *specifier*

The abbreviation of an element begins with an optional specifier. The name specified appears to the right of the optional specifier followed by the keyword **IS**, the abbreviated element appears to the right of the keyword **IS**. The line on which the abbreviation occurs may be broken after the keyword **IS** or at some valid point in the element. The type of the element must be the same as the type of the specifier. As for abbreviations of values, the specifier can usually be omitted from the abbreviation, as the type can be inferred from the type of the element. A specifier **[]** *type* simply defines the abbreviation as being an array with components of the specified type.

9.3   Disjoint arrays in parallels

Abbreviations may be used to decompose an array into a number of disjoint parts, so that each part may have a unique name in all or several processes in parallel. Components of each disjoint part may then be selected by a variable subscript (a subscript whose value is dependent on a procedure parameter, a variable, or a replicator index whose base or count is not a constant value), for example:

```
frame1 IS [page FROM 0 FOR 512] :
frame2 IS [page FROM 512 FOR 512] :
PAR
  INT i :
  SEQ
    ...
    c1 ? frame1[i]
    ...
  INT j :
  SEQ
    ...
    c2 ? frame2[j]
    ...
```

This example divides the array **page** into two parts, and provides a name for those parts in each of the two parallel processes. These parts may then be selected by using variable subscripts.

10 Procedures

This chapter describes *procedures* in occam. A procedure definition in occam defines a name for a process. Consider the following example:

```
PROC increment (INT x)
  x := x + 1
:
```

This example defines **increment** as the name for the process, **x := x + 1**. *Formal parameters* of a procedure are specified in parentheses after the procedure name. In this example, **x** is a formal parameter, and is of type **INT**. The procedure **increment** may be used as shown in the following example:

```
INT y :
SEQ
  ...
  increment (y)
  ...
```

A formal parameter is an *abbreviation* (page 57) of the *actual parameter* used in an *instance* of a procedure. An *instance* of a procedure has the same effect as the substitution of the process named in the procedure's definition. This instance of **increment** can be expanded to show its effect:

```
INT y :
SEQ
  ...
  x IS y :
  x := x + 1
  ...
```

which is equivalent to

```
INT y :
SEQ
  ...
  y := y + 1
  ...
```

Here is a further example:

```
PROC writes (CHAN OF BYTE stream, VAL []BYTE string)
  SEQ i = 0 FOR SIZE string
    stream ! string[i]
:
```

This procedure takes a channel (**stream**) and an array (**string**) as parameters, and outputs the components of the array to the channel. An instance of the procedure looks like this:

```
SEQ
  ...
  writes (screen, "Hello world")
  ...
```

Again, this instance can be expanded to show the effect:

```
SEQ
  ...
  CHAN OF BYTE stream IS screen :
  VAL []BYTE string IS "Hello world" :
  SEQ i = 0 FOR SIZE string
    stream ! string[i]
  ...
```

The rules for procedure parameters follow from those for abbreviations. There are two kinds of abbreviation: abbreviations which specify a name for the value of an *expression* (page 43), and abbreviations which specify a name for an *element* (page 39) of an existing *variable, channel, timer,* or *array*. Abbreviations have already been discussed in chapter 9 which starts on page 57. A name which is *free* in the body of the procedure is statically bound to the name used in the procedure definition, for example:

```
INT step :
SEQ
  step := 39
  PROC next.item (INT next, VAL INT present)
    next := present + step
  :
  INT g, step :
  SEQ
    step := 7
    next.item (g, 3)
    ...           -- at this point the value of g is 42
```

The free variable **step**, in scope when the procedure **next.item** was defined, is *bound* to the procedure **next.item**. The rules of occam state that all names identify distinct objects. In the example, the scope and binding of the elements can be seen more clearly by making systematic changes of name. Once this is done, the example is equivalent to:

```
INT step :
SEQ
  step := 39
  INT g, curb :   -- name changed
  SEQ
    curb := 7
    next IS g :   -- expand instance of next.item
    VAL present IS 3 :
    next := present + step
    ...           -- at this point the value of g is 42
```

In this transformation of the earlier example, it can be seen that the variable used in the instance of **next.item** is the variable named **step** declared before the procedure definition of **next.item**, and not the second variable declared with the same name. Consider this example:

```
INT x, y, step :
PROC next.item (INT next, VAL INT present)
  next := present + step
:
```

And now consider the following equivalences of instances that may appear in the scope of the procedure:

next.item (x, y)	is equivalent to:	`INT next IS x :`
		`VAL INT present IS y :`
		`next := present + step`

next.item (x, step)	is equivalent to:	`INT next IS x :`
		`VAL INT present IS step :`
		`next := present + step`

next.item (step, x)	is equivalent to:
	which is **INVALID!**
		`INT next IS step :`
		`VAL INT present IS x :`
		`next := present + step`

next.item (x, x)	is equivalent to:
	which is **INVALID!**
		`INT next IS x :`
		`VAL INT present IS x :`
		`next := present + step`

Here it can be seen how the meaning of each procedure parameter is defined in terms of an abbreviation, the ordering of parameters corresponds to a sequence of abbreviations. **next.item (step, x)** is invalid because the element **step** is used in the expression **next := present + step**, after it has been abbreviated, and the example `next.item (x, x)` is invalid as **x** has already been used in the previous abbreviation of the element **x** (and the rules state [abbreviations on page 57] that an element used in such an abbreviation may not be used within the associated scope). Notice also the effect with the order of parameters used in `next.item` changed:

```
INT x, y, step :
PROC next.item (VAL INT present, INT next)
  next := present + step
:
```

With this re-ordering, `next.item (x, x)` is still invalid, although now for a different reason, as follows:

```
next.item (x, x)   is equivalent to:    VAL INT present IS x :
                   which is INVALID!    INT next IS x :
                                        next := present + step
```

`next.item (x, x)` is invalid here as there is an assignment to **x** (via **next**) within the scope of the first abbreviation. Now consider the following example:

```
PROC nonsense (INT x, VAL INT y)
  SEQ
    x := x + y
    x := x - y
:
```

This procedure should leave the value of the variable used as the actual parameter for **x**, unchanged, as the following expansion shows:

```
nonsense (n, 3)   is equivalent to:    INT x IS n :
                                       VAL INT y IS 3 :
                                       SEQ
                                         x := x + y
                                         x := x - y
```
```
                  and by substitution  SEQ
                                         n := n + 3
                                         n := n - 3
```

The value of **n** after this instance is **n**, as might be expected. However, the following instance is invalid, which is just as well, as the effect is non-intuitive:

```
nonsense (n, n)   is equivalent to:    INT x IS n :
                  which is INVALID!    VAL INT y IS n :
                                       SEQ
                                         x := x + y
                                         x := x - y
```
```
                  and by substitution  SEQ
                  a non-intuitive effect!  n := n + n
                                         n := n - n
```

The value of **n** after this instance, if it were valid, would be 0, which is counter intuitive. The following example highlights the problem further.

```
nonsense (i, v[i])    is equivalent to:    INT x IS i :
                      which is INVALID!    VAL INT y IS v[i] :
                                           SEQ
                                             x := x + y
                                             x := x - y

                      and by substitution   SEQ
                      a non-intuitive effect!   i := i + v[i]
                                                i := i - v[i]
```

If this instance were valid, the value of **i** after the instance of **nonsense** would be difficult to predict, as in each of the assignments **v[i]** will probably reference a different component of **v**, as the value of the subscript **i** may be changed by the first assignment.

The syntax for a procedure definition is:

```
definition       =      PROC name ( {₀ , formal } )
                            procedure.body
                        :
formal           =      specifier {₁ , name }
                 |      VAL specifier {₁ , name }
procedure.body   =      process
```

The keyword **PROC**, the name of the procedure, and a formal parameter list enclosed in parentheses is followed by a process, indented two spaces, which is the body of the procedure. The procedure definition is terminated by a colon which appears on a new line at the same indentation level as the start of the definition.

The syntax for procedure instance is:

```
instance   =      name ( {₀ , actual } )
actual     =      element
           |      expression
```

An instance of a procedure is the procedure name followed by a list of zero or more actual parameters in parentheses. An actual parameter is either an element or expression. The list of actual parameters must correspond directly to the list of formal parameters used in the definition of the procedure. The actual parameter list must have the same number of entries, each of which must be the compatible with the kind (**VAL** or non-**VAL**) and type of the corresponding formal parameter. In a program in which all names are distinct, an instance of a procedure behaves like the substitution of the procedure body. Notice that all programs can be expressed in a form in which all names are made distinct by systematic changes of name. Procedures in occam 2 are not recursive. A channel parameter or free channel may only be used for input or output (not both) in the procedure.

An instance of a procedure defined with zero parameters must be followed by empty parentheses. Where a number of parameters of the same type appear in the parameter list, a single specifier may specify several names. For example:

```
PROC snark (VAL INT butcher, beaver, REAL64 boojum, jubjub)
  ...
:
```

This example, is equivalent to:

```
PROC snark (VAL INT butcher, VAL INT beaver,
            REAL64 boojum,    REAL64 jubjub)
  ...
:
```

11 Functions

The previous chapter discusses named processes (called *procedures*). This chapter describes *functions* in occam. A function defines a name for a special kind of process, called a *value process*. A value process produces a result of primitive data type (but not of array type), and may appear in expressions. Value processes may also produce more than one result, which may be assigned in a multiple assignment. occam functions are side effect free, as they are forbidden to communicate or assign to free variables. This helps to ensure that programs are clear and easy to maintain.

A value process, performs an enclosed process, and produces a result. Consider the following example:

```
total := subtotal + (INT sum :
                     VALOF
                       SEQ
                         sum := 0
                         SEQ i = 0 FOR SIZE v
                           sum := sum + v[i]
                       RESULT sum
                     )
```

In the example shown here, the value process produces the sum of the array **v**, and is equivalent to

$$(\sum_{i=0}^{SIZE v} v[i])$$

More commonly however, the value process is the body of a function definition, as illustrated in the following example:

```
INT FUNCTION sum (VAL []INT values)
  INT accumulator :
  VALOF
    SEQ
      accumulator := 0
      SEQ i = 0 FOR SIZE values
        accumulator := accumulator + values[i]
    RESULT accumulator
:
```

This function definition defines the name **sum** for the associated value process. The type of the result is **INT**, specified by **INT FUNCTION**. Just as the behaviour of procedures is defined by the substitution of the procedure body, functions behave like the substitution of the function body. It follows that the example which starts this chapter is an expansion of the following:

```
total := subtotal + sum (v)
```

A function definition may also define a name for an expression list, so that simple, single line, functions can be defined in the following fashion:

```
BOOL FUNCTION lowercase (VAL BYTE ch) IS (ch >= 'a') AND (ch <= 'z') :
BOOL FUNCTION uppercase (VAL BYTE ch) IS (ch >= 'A') AND (ch <= 'Z') :
BOOL FUNCTION ischar (VAL BYTE ch) IS uppercase (ch) OR lowercase (ch) :
```

Each of these functions returns a single boolean result. The definition of the function **ischar** is equivalent to the following:

```
BOOL FUNCTION ischar (VAL BYTE ch)
  VALOF
    SKIP
    RESULT uppercase (ch) OR lowercase (ch)
:
```

A number of rules apply to functions to ensure they are side effect free. As for procedures, the correspondence between the formal and actual parameters of a function is defined in terms of *abbreviations*, and follows the associated scope rules. However, an argument of a function may only be a value parameter. Only variables declared within the scope of a value process or function may be assigned to. Also, value processes may not contain inputs or outputs, nor may they contain alternations, or parallels. The body of any procedure used within a function must also obey the above rules. A name which is free within the value process (Scope, page 53) can be used only in expressions within the value process or function body, they may not be assigned to by input or assignment. Consider the following:

```
INT FUNCTION read.top.of.stack () IS stack[stack.pointer] :
BOOL FUNCTION empty () IS stack.pointer = 0 :
```

A value process may produce more than one result, which may then be assigned using a multiple assignment. Consider the following example:

```
point, found := (VAL BYTE char IS 'g' :
                 VAL []BYTE string IS message :
                 BOOL ok :
                 INT ptr :
                 VALOF
                   IF
                     IF i = 0 FOR SIZE string
                       string[i] = char
                         SEQ
                           ok := TRUE
                           ptr := i
                     TRUE
                       SEQ
                         ok := FALSE
                         ptr := -1
                   RESULT ptr, ok
                 )
```

This value process searches the byte array **string** for the character **'g'**. The result is produced from the expression list which follows **RESULT**, and is then assigned to **point**, and **found**. This value process can be given a name in a function definition, as follows:

```
INT, BOOL FUNCTION instr (VAL BYTE char, VAL []BYTE string)
  BOOL ok :
  INT ptr :
  VALOF
    IF
      IF i = 0 FOR SIZE string
        string[i] = char
          SEQ
            ok := TRUE
            ptr := i
      TRUE
        SEQ
          ok := FALSE
          ptr := -1
    RESULT ptr, ok
  :
VAL message IS "Twas brillig and the slithy toves" :
INT point :
BOOL found :
SEQ
  point, found := instr ("g", message)
  ...
```

This example finds the position of **g** in the string **message**. After the multiple assignment in this example, the value of **point** will be 11, and the value of found will be **TRUE**. Single line functions with multiple results may also be defined:

```
INT, INT FUNCTION div.rem (VAL INT x, y) IS x / y, x REM y :
```

This function produces the division, and remainder of **x** and **y**. If an error occurs within a function or value process, it will behave like the primitive process **STOP**. This behaviour is equivalent to the behaviour of a mathematical overflow in an arithmetic expression (see page 78 for details of the behaviour of invalid processes). Consider the behaviour of an instance of the following partial function:

```
INT FUNCTION factorial (VAL INT n)
  INT product :
  VALOF
    IF
      n >= 0
        SEQ
          product := 1
          SEQ i = 1 FOR n
            product := product * i
    RESULT product
```

This function will behave like the primitive process **STOP** if **n** is less than zero, or if an overflow occurs in the evaluation of the factorial. In either case the behaviour is equivalent to the behaviour of any other invalid expression (page 78).

The syntax for functions is:

value.process	=	*valof*
valof	=	**VALOF**
		process
		RESULT *expression.list*
	|	*specification*
		valof
operand	=	(*value.process*
		)
expression.list	=	(*value.process*
		)
definition	=	$\{_1$, *primitive.type* } **FUNCTION** *name* ($\{_0$, *formal* })
		function.body
		:
function.body	=	*value.process*
operand	=	*name* ($\{_0$, *expression* })
expression.list	=	*name* ($\{_0$, *expression* })
definition	=	$\{_1$, *primitive.type* } **FUNCTION** *name* ($\{_0$, *formal* }) **IS** *expression.list* :

A value process consists of zero or more specifications which precede the keyword **VALOF**, followed by a process at an indentation of two spaces, and the keyword **RESULT** at the same indentation. The keyword **RESULT** is followed by an expression list on the same line. The line may be broken after a comma, or at a valid point in an expression. An operand of an expression may consist of a left parentheses, a value process, followed by a right parentheses. The structured parentheses appear at the same indentation as each other, and are equivalent to the left hand and right hand parentheses of a bracketed expression respectively. So, where the value process produces a single result, the upper bracket may be preceded by an operator, or the lower bracket may be followed by an operator.

The heading of a function definition consists of the keyword **FUNCTION**, preceded by the type(s) of the result(s) produced by the function. The name of the function and a formal parameter list enclosed by parentheses follows the keyword **FUNCTION** on the same line. This is followed by a value process, indented two spaces, which forms the body of the function. The function definition is terminated by a colon which appears on a new line at the same indentation level as the start of the definition. Alternatively, a function definition may consist of the function heading followed by the keyword **IS**, an expression list, and a colon, on the same line. The line may be broken after the keyword **IS**, a comma, or at a valid point in an expression.

An instance of a function defined to have zero parameters must be followed by empty parentheses. Where a number of parameters of the same type appear in the parameter list, a single specifier may specify several names. For example:

```
INT FUNCTION alice (VAL REAL64 tweedle.dum, tweedle.dee,
                    VAL INT cheshire.cat)
  . . .
:
```

This example, is equivalent to:

```
INT FUNCTION alice (VAL REAL64 tweedle.dum,
                    VAL REAL64 tweedle.dee,
                    VAL INT cheshire.cat)
  . . .
:
```

Appendices

This appendix describes the aspects of occam which specify the *configuration* of an occam program. Configuration associates the components of an occam program with a set of physical resources. During configuration the processes which make up an occam program are distributed over the number of interconnected processing devices available in the environment in which the program will execute. The processes which execute on a single processor may be given a priority of execution, and the channels which interconnect the distributed processes may be mapped onto the physical communication links between processing devices. It is expected that the program is logically correct before configuration is used to optimise performance. Configuration does not affect the logical behaviour of a program.

A.1   Execution on multiple processors

The component processes of a parallel may each be executed on an individual processor. This can be specified by a *placed parallel* which assigns a process for execution on a specified processor. Consider the following example:

```
PLACED PAR
   PROCESSOR 1
      terminal (term.in, term.out)
   PROCESSOR 2
      editor (term.in, term.out, files.in, files.out)
   PROCESSOR 3
      network (files.in, files.out)
```

In this example, the processes **terminal**, **editor** and **network**, are placed on three individual processors numbered **1**, **2** and **3**. Each process is executed on the assigned processor, each process uses local memory, and communicates with the other processes via channels.

The syntax for a placed par is:

placedpar   =   **PLACED PAR**
                        { *placedpar* }
               | **PLACED PAR** *replicator*
                        placedpar
               | **PROCESSOR** *expression*
                        process
parallel   =   *placedpar*

The keywords **PLACED PAR** are followed by zero or more processor allocations. A processor allocation is the keyword **PROCESSOR**, and an expression of type **INT** which serves to identify the processor on which the associated process is to be placed. As for normal parallels (page 16), the placed parallel may be replicated. An implementation may extend this syntax to identify the type of processor on which the process is placed. All variables and timers used within the placement must be declared within it.

A.2   Execution priority on a single processor

A.2.1   Priority parallel

The component processes of a parallel (page 15) executing on a single processor may be assigned a priority of execution. Consider the following example:

```
PRI PAR
   terminal (term.in, term.out)
   editor   (term.in, term.out)
```

This process will always execute the process **terminal** in preference to the process **editor**. Each process executes at a separate priority, the first process is the highest priority, the last is the lowest. Lower priority processes may only continue when all higher priority processes are unable to. The process may also be replicated, as shown in the following example:

```
PRI PAR i = 0 FOR 8
  users (term.in[i], term.out[i])
```

The process with the highest index is executed at the lowest priority.

The syntax for priority execution is:

parallel =   **PRI PAR**
                      { *process* }
                 | **PRI PAR** *replicator*
                      process

The keywords **PRI PAR** are followed by zero or more processes at an indentation of two spaces. As for parallels detailed in the main body of the manual (page 16), the process may be replicated.

A.2.2   Priority alternation

The inputs which guard alternatives in an alternation (page 18) may also be given a selection priority. Consider the following example:

```
PRI ALT
  disk ? block
    d ()
  keyboard ? char
    k ()
```

This priority alternation will input values from the channel **disk** in preference to inputs from the channel **keyboard**. If both channels **disk** and **keyboard** become ready then **disk** will be selected as it has the highest priority.

Consider the following example:

```
PRI ALT
  stream ? data
    P ()
  busy & SKIP
    Q ()
```

This process inputs **data** if an input from **stream** is ready, and performs the process **P**, otherwise if the boolean **busy** is true the process **Q** is performed.

The syntax for priority alternation is:

alternation =   **PRI ALT**
                         { *alternative* }
                    | **PRI ALT** *replicator*
                         alternative

The keywords **PRI ALT** are followed by zero or more processes at an indentation of two spaces. As for alternations detailed earlier in the manual (page 20) the alternative may be replicated.

A.3   Allocation to memory

This section explains how a *variable*, *channel*, *timer* or *array* may be placed at an absolute location in memory. occam presents a consistent view of a processor's memory map. Memory is considered to be an array of type **INT**, each address in memory is considered a subscript into that array. Consider the following example:

```
PLACE term.in AT linklin :
```

This allocation places the element **term.in** at the location specified by **linklin**. Here are some further examples:

```
[80]INT buffer :
PLACE buffer AT #0400 :

[5]REAL32 points :
PLACE points AT #0800 :

CHAN OF INT term.out :
PLACE term.out AT 3 :
```

The syntax for allocation is:

process	=	*allocation* :
		process
allocation	=	**PLACE** *name* **AT** *expression* :

An allocation begins with the keyword **PLACE**, followed by the name of the variable, channel, timer or array to be placed. This in turn is followed by an expression of type **INT** which indicates the absolute location in memory.

An allocation must allocate an element to a compatible location. That is, a timer should be placed at a location which acts as a timer, and a channel should be placed at the location which implements a channel. Also, arrays must not be placed so that the components of an array overlap other allocations.

This appendix describes how memory mapped devices may be addressed in occam. A process may communicate with external devices which are mapped into the processor's memory map, using a special input or output in a way similar to communication on channels. A special type declares a *port* which must then be placed using an allocation (page 73). Consider the following example:

```
PORT OF INT16 status :
PLACE status AT uart.status :
SEQ
    . . .
    status ? state
    status ! reset
    . . .
```

This example declares a port which is then allocated to a location **uart.status** in memory. The following sequence includes an input which reads the value of the port, and also an output which writes a value **reset** to the port location. Consider the following examples of port declarations:

`PORT OF [8]INT uart :`	one port of type `[8]INT`
`[8]PORT OF BYTE transducer :`	eight ports of byte type

A port declaration is similar to a channel declaration, and must obey the same rules of scope (page 53). That is, a port may not be used for input or output in more than one component process in a parallel.

The syntax for ports is:

primitive.type	=	**PORT OF** *type*
port	=	*element*
input	=	*port* **?** *variable*
output	=	*port* **!** *expression*

The syntax shows that ports are a primitive type, just like data types, channels and timers. A port is declared in just the same way as a channel. Instead of a defined *protocol* (page 29) the port definition specifies a type, which must be a data type, as the type for communication.

This appendix summarises the rules which govern the use of variables, channels, timers, ports (page 74) and arrays in parallel constructions, and the rules which govern abbreviations and parameters. These rules are discussed in context throughout the manual, and are gathered here as a check list.

C.1   Usage in parallel

The purpose of these rules is to prevent parallel processes from sharing variables, to ensure that each channel connects only two parallel processes, and to ensure that the connection of channels is unidirectional. The rules allow most of the checking for valid usage to be performed by a compiler, thus reducing runtime overheads.

A channel implements a point-to-point communication between two parallel processes. The name of a channel may only be used in one component of a parallel for input, and in one other component of the parallel for output.

A timer may be used for input by any number of components of a parallel.

A variable or component of an array of variables, which is assigned to in a component of a parallel, may not appear in any other component of the parallel.

An array may be used in more than one component of a parallel, if and only if the subscripts used to select components of the array can be determined at compile time. Otherwise the array may only be used in one component of the parallel.

Several abbreviations can decompose an array into non-overlapping disjoint parts; components of these parts may then be selected using variable subscripts.

A port may be used in only one component of a parallel.

C.2   The rules for abbreviations

The purpose of these rules is to ensure that each name identifies a unique object, and that the substitution semantics are maintained.

All reference to an abbreviated element must be via the abbreviation only, with the exception that array elements may be further abbreviated providing the later abbreviations do not include components of the array already abbreviated.

Variables used in an abbreviated expression may not be assigned to by input or assignment within the scope of the abbreviation.

The abbreviated expression must be valid, i.e. in range and not subject to overflow, and all subscript expressions must be in range.

All subscript expressions used in an element abbreviation must be valid, i.e. not subject to overflow and in range.

All reference to a *retyped* element must be via the new name only, with the exception that array elements may be further retyped providing the later retyping conversions do not include components of the array already retyped.

Variables used in a retyping conversion may not be assigned to by input or assignment within the scope of the new name.

C.3   The rules for procedures

The rules for procedure parameters follow from those for abbreviations, but in addition a channel parameter or free channel may not be used for both input or output in a procedure.

C.4   The rules for value processes and functions

Functions may only have value parameters.

Only variables declared within the scope of a value process may be assigned to. Free names may be used in expressions.

A value process may not contain inputs, outputs, parallels or alternations.

The body of a procedure used within a function must also obey these rules.

This appendix describes retyping conversion. A retyping conversion changes the data type of a bit pattern, from one data type to another. There are two kinds of retyping conversions: conversions which convert an element, and conversions which convert the value of an expression. The length (i.e. the number of bits) of the new type specified must be the same as the length of the bit pattern. A retyping conversion has no effect upon the bit pattern, and differs from *type conversion* (page 49) where the value of one type is represented as an equivalent value of another type.

The retyping conversion of a value may be used to specify a name for a particular bit pattern described by a hexadecimal constant. Consider the following example:

```
VAL REAL32 root.NaN RETYPES #7F840000(INT32) :
```

The advantage of the above conversion is that it has been possible to specify the exact representation of a value otherwise difficult to represent. Consider also the following example:

```
VAL INT64 pattern RETYPES 42.0(REAL64) :
```

The bit pattern for the real representation of the value 42.0 is mapped to a name **pattern** of type **INT64**. As for the *abbreviations* (page 57) of expressions, no variable used in the expression may be assigned to by input or assignment within the scope of the conversion.

The retyping conversion may also specify a name of a new type for an existing element of the same length. For example:

```
INT64 condition :
  . . .
    [8]BYTE state RETYPES condition :
    . . .
```

In this example, **condition**, a variable of type **INT64**, is converted into an array of 8 bytes. Each byte is accessible via subscript, any change to the bit pattern as a result of an assignment or input will directly affect the value of the original element.

The same rules apply to names specified by retyping conversions as apply to abbreviations. That is, no variable used in a subscript or count expression which selects a component or segment of an array may be assigned to by an input or assignment within the *scope* (page 53, the region of a program where a name is valid) of the conversion. The element converted may not be be used within the scope of the conversion. See the rules which affect abbreviations on page 58.

The syntax for retyping conversion is:

> *definition*   =   *specifier name* **RETYPES** *element* :
> | **VAL** *specifier name* **RETYPES** *expression* :

The retyping conversion of a value begins with the keyword **VAL**, a specifier appears to the right of **VAL**, followed by the name specified, and the keyword **RETYPES**, the expression appears to the right of the keyword **RETYPES**. The line on which the conversion occurs may not be broken after the keyword **RETYPES**, but may be broken at some valid point in the expression.

As word alignment tends to vary between machines, the use of retyping conversion will normally result in implementation dependent processes.

Processes which become invalid during program execution may behave in one of three ways, determined by a compiler option. An invalid process may behave in one of these ways: the process may stop, the system may halt, or the behaviour of the process may be undefined.

The three modes of existence in detail are:

Stop process mode In this mode, processes which become invalid behave like the primitive process **STOP**, thus allowing other processes to continue. The invalid process stops, and in particular does not make erroneous outputs to other processes. Other processes continue until they become dependent upon data from the stopped process. In this mode it is therefore possible to write communications which will timeout to warn of a stopped process, and to construct a system with redundancy in which a number of processes performing the same task may be used to enable the system to continue after one of the processes has failed.

Halt system mode In this mode an invalid process may cause the whole system to halt, and is useful for the development of programs, particularly when debugging concurrent systems. In this mode the primitive process **STOP** will also cause the whole system to halt.

Undefined mode In this mode, an invalid process may have an arbitrary effect, and is only useful for optimising programs known to be correct!

Earlier sections of this manual have discussed rounding and the possibilty of rounding errors. These occur because the types **REAL32** and **REAL64** only contain a subset of the real numbers. This is because it is not possible to store all the possible real values in the format for real numbers available on a machine. Rounding takes a value, which is considered infinitely precise and, if necessary, modifies it to a value which is representable by the type. By default, values are rounded to the nearest value of the type, if the nearest greater value and the nearest smaller value are equally near, then the result which has the least significant bit zero is chosen. Other modes of rounding are selectable using the **IEEEOP** library routine, these modes round values toward plus infinity, minus infinity or toward zero. A value rounded to plus infinity is the value nearest to and not less than the value to be represented, a value rounded to minus infinity is the value nearest to and not greater than the value to be represented, a value rounded toward zero is the value no greater in magnitude than the value to be represented.

A value is rounded to the precision of its type. A value of type **REAL32** is equivalent to IEEE single precision, and a value of type **REAL64** is equivalent to IEEE double precision.

Values in the **REAL32** and **REAL64** formats are stored in the following formats

s	exp	frac

where *s* is the sign bit, *exp* is the exponent and *frac* is the fraction. For the **REAL32** type *s* is 1 bit wide, *exp* is 8 bits wide and *frac* is 23 bits wide. For the **REAL64** type *s* is 1 bit wide, *exp* is 11 bits wide and *frac* is 52 bits wide. Whenever the *exp* field is not 0 the actual fraction of the number represented has an "implied" 1 placed on the left of the *frac* value.

The value of finite **REAL**s is given by

$$val \boxed{s \mid exp \mid frac} = \begin{cases} (-1)^s \times 1.frac \times 2^{exp-bias}, & \text{if } exp \neq 0; \\ (-1)^s \times 0.frac \times 2^{1-bias}, & \text{if } exp = 0; \end{cases}$$

where *bias* is 127 for **REAL32** and 1023 for **REAL64**

In the **REAL32** type the value 1.0 is represented by an unset sign bit *s*, an *exp* equal to 127, and a *frac* of 0. The next larger number has an unset signbit, *exp* of 127 and a *frac* of 1. This has the value 1.00000019209..... Hence any number lying between 1.0 and this value cannot be exactly represented in the **REAL32** type – such values have to be *rounded* to one of these values. Now consider the assignment:

```
X := 1.0(REAL32) + 1.0E-7(REAL32)
```

The previous sections show that the result of this operation cannot be exactly represented by the type **REAL32**. The exact result has to be rounded to "fit" the type. Here the exact result will be rounded to the nearest **REAL32** value 1.00000019209...

Other rounding modes – Round to Zero (truncation), Round to Plus infinity and Round to Minus infinity – can be obtained through the use of the **IEEEOP** function. Because of the presence of rounding, programmers should be wary of using equality tests on real types. Consider the following example:

```
SEQ
    X := 1.0(REAL32)
    WHILE X <> 1.000001(REAL32)
        X := X + 0.0000005(REAL32)
```

never terminates as rounding errors cause `1.000001` and `1.0 + 0.0000005 + 0.0000005` to differ.

The nearest unique value of a conversion of a literal of type **REAL32** can be determined from the first 9 significant digits, and from the first 17 significant digits of a literal of type **REAL64**. Complete details of the IEEE Standard for Binary Floating-Point Arithmetic can be found in the published ANSI/IEEE Std 754-1985 standard.

G.1   Syntax in context

The following tables present the syntax of occam 2. Each syntactic object appears in context. However,
the following BNF should not be read in isolation. The syntactic objects are kept to a minimum, and must
be considered in association with the semantic rules given in the definition. Thus, for example, the use of
primitive.type and *type* in the syntax

   simple.protocol   =   *primitive.type*: : [ ] *type*

is clarified by the semantics which point out that the *primitive.type* must be an integer or byte type, and that
type must be a data type.

G.1.1   Processes

process	=	**SKIP** | **STOP**
	|	*action*
	|	*construction*
	|	*instance*
action	=	*assignment* | *input* | *output*
assignment	=	*variable* : = *expression*
input	=	*channel* ? *variable*
output	=	*channel* ! *expression*
assignment	=	*variable.list* : = *expression.list*
variable.list	=	{₁ , *variable* }
expression.list	=	{₁ , *expression* }

G.1.2   Construction

construction	=	*sequence* | *conditional* | *selection* | *loop*
	|	*parallel* | *alternation*
sequence	=	**SEQ** { *process* }
conditional	=	**IF** { *choice* }
choice	=	*guarded.choice* | *conditional*
guarded.choice	=	*boolean* *process*
boolean	=	*expression*
selection	=	**CASE** *selector* { *option* }
option	=	{₁ , *case.expression* } *process*
	|	**ELSE** *process*
selector	=	*expression*
case.expression	=	*expression*
loop	=	**WHILE** *boolean* *process*
parallel	=	**PAR** { *process* }

```
alternation          =      ALT
                             {  alternative  }
alternative          =      guarded.alternative  |  alternation
guarded.alternative  =      guard
                               process
guard                =      input
                       |    boolean & input
                       |    boolean & SKIP
```

G.1.3   Replicator

```
sequence     =    SEQ replicator
                    process
conditional  =    IF replicator
                    choice
parallel     =    PAR replicator
                    process
alternation  =    ALT replicator
                    alternative
replicator   =    name = base FOR count
base         =    expression
count        =    expression
```

G.1.4   Types

```
type            =         primitive.type
                    |     array.type
primitive.type  =         CHAN OF protocol
                    |     TIMER
                    |     BOOL
                    |     BYTE
                    |     INT
                    |     INT16
                    |     INT32
                    |     INT64
                    |     REAL32
                    |     REAL64
array.type      =         [ expression ] type
```

G.1.5   Literal

```
literal     =      integer
              |    byte
              |    integer ( type )
              |    byte ( type )
              |    real ( type )
              |    string
              |    TRUE | FALSE
integer     =    digits | #hex.digits
byte        =    ' character'
real        =    digits . digits | digits . digitsEexponent
exponent    =    +digits | −digits
digit       =    0 | 1 | 2 | 3 | 4 | 5 | 6 | 7 | 8 | 9
hex.digit   =    digit | A | B | C | D | E | F
```

G.1.6   Declaration

declaration =   *type* {₁ , *name* } :

G.1.7   Protocol

definition	=	**PROTOCOL** *name* **IS** *simple.protocol* :
	|	**PROTOCOL** *name* **IS** *sequential.protocol* :
protocol	=	*name*

simple.protocol	=	*type*
	|	*primitive.type* : : [ ] *type*
input	=	*channel* ? *input.item*
input.item	=	*variable*
	|	*variable* : : *variable*
output	=	*channel* ! *output.item*
output.item	=	*expression*
	|	*expression* : : *expression*
protocol	=	*simple.protocol*

sequential.protocol	=	{₁ ; *simple.protocol* }
input	=	*channel* ? {₁ ; *input.item* }
output	=	*channel* ! {₁ ; *output.item* }

definition	=	**PROTOCOL** *name*
		CASE
		{ *tagged.protocol* }
		:
tagged.protocol	=	*tag*
	|	*tag* ; *sequential.protocol*
tag	=	*name*

| *output* | = | *channel* ! *tag* |
| | \| | *channel* ! *tag* ; {₁ ; *output.item* } |

case.input	=	*channel* ? **CASE**
		{ *variant* }
variant	=	*tagged.list*
		process
	|	*specification*
		variant
tagged.list	=	*tag*
	|	*tag* ; {₁ ; *input.item* }
process	=	*case.input*
input	=	*channel* ? **CASE** *tagged.list*

alternative	=	*channel* ? **CASE**
		{ *variant* }
	|	*boolean* **&** *channel* ? **CASE**
		{ *variant* }

G.1.8   Timer access

input	=	*timer.input*
	|	*delayed.input*
timer.input	=	*timer* ? *variable*
delayed.input	=	*timer* ? **AFTER** *expression*

G.1.9   Element

element	=	*element* [*subscript*]
	|	[*element* **FROM** *subscript* **FOR** *count*]
	|	*name*
subscript	=	*expression*
variable	=	*element*
channel	=	*element*
timer	=	*element*

G.1.10   Expression

operand	=	*element*
	|	*literal*
	|	*table*
	|	(*expression*)
expression	=	*monadic.operator operand*
	|	*operand dyadic.operator operand*
	|	*conversion*
	|	*operand*
table	=	*table* [*subscript*]
	|	[{$_1$, *expression* }]
	|	[*table* **FROM** *subscript* **FOR** *count*]
expression	=	**MOSTPOS** *type*
	|	**MOSTNEG** *type*
conversion	=	*primitive.type operand*
	|	*primitive.type* **ROUND** *operand*
	|	*primitive.type* **TRUNC** *operand*

G.1.11   Abbreviation

abbreviation	=	*specifier name* **IS** *element* :
	|	*name* **IS** *element* :
	|	**VAL** *specifier name* **IS** *expression* :
	|	**VAL** *name* **IS** *expression* :
specifier	=	*primitive.type*
	|	[] *specifier*
	|	[*expression*] *specifier*

G.1.12   Scope

process	=	*specification*
		process
choice	=	*specification*
		choice
option	=	*specification*
		option
alternative	=	*specification*
		alternative
variant	=	*specification*
		variant
valof	=	*specification*
		valof
specification	=	*declaration* | *abbreviation* | *definition*

G.1.13   Procedure

definition	=	**PROC** *name* ($\{_0$, *formal* })
		procedure.body
		:
formal	=	*specifier* $\{_1$, *name* }
		| **VAL** *specifier* $\{_1$, *name* }
procedure.body	=	*process*
instance	=	*name* ($\{_0$, *actual* })
actual	=	*element*
		| *expression*

G.1.14   Function

value.process	=	*valof*
valof	=	**VALOF**
		process
		RESULT *expression.list*
		| *specification*
		valof
operand	=	(*value.process*
		)
expression.list	=	(*value.process*
		)
definition	=	$\{_1$, *primitive.type* } **FUNCTION** *name* ($\{_0$, *formal* })
		function.body
		:
function.body	=	*value.process*
operand	=	*name* ($\{_0$, *expression* })
expression.list	=	*name* ($\{_0$, *expression* })
definition	=	$\{_1$, *primitive.type* } **FUNCTION** *name* ($\{_0$, *formal* }) **IS** *expression.list* :

G.1.15   Configuration

placedpar	=	**PLACED PAR**
		{ *placedpar* }
	|	**PLACED PAR** *replicator*
		placedpar
	|	**PROCESSOR** *expression*
		process
parallel	=	*placedpar*
parallel	=	**PRI PAR**
		{ *process* }
	|	**PRI PAR** *replicator*
		process
alternation	=	**PRI ALT**
		{ *alternative* }
	|	**PRI ALT** *replicator*
		alternative
process	=	*allocation*
		process
allocation	=	**PLACE** *name* **AT** *expression* :
definition	=	*specifier name* **RETYPES** *element* :
	|	**VAL** *specifier name* **RETYPES** *expression* :
primitive.type	=	**PORT OF** *type*
port	=	*element*
input	=	*port* ? *variable*
output	=	*port* ! *expression*
protocol	=	**ANY**

G.2   Ordered syntax

The following tables present the syntax of occam with each syntactic object placed in alphabetical order.

    abbreviation =   specifier name IS element :
                  | name IS element :
                  | VAL specifier name IS expression :
                  | VAL name IS expression :

    action =   assignment
            | input
            | output

    actual =   element
            | expression

    allocation =   PLACE name AT expression :

    alternation =   ALT
                      { alternative }
                 | ALT replicator
                      alternative
                 | PRI ALT
                      { alternative }
                 | PRI ALT replicator
                      alternative

    alternative =   guarded.alternative | alternation
                 | specification
                      alternative
                 | channel ? CASE
                      { variant }
                 | boolean & channel ? CASE
                      { variant }

    array.type =   [expression] type

    assignment =   variable := expression
                | variable.list := expression.list

    base =   expression

    boolean =   expression

    byte =   ' character'

    case.expression =   expression

    case.input =   channel ? CASE
                     { variant }

    channel =   element

    choice =   guarded.choice | conditional
            | specification
                 choice

conditional = **IF**
{ *choice* }
| **IF** *replicator*
choice

construction = *sequence* | *conditional* | *selection* | *loop*
| *parallel* | *alternation*

conversion = *primitive.type operand*
| *primitive.type* **ROUND** *operand*
| *primitive.type* **TRUNC** *operand*

count = *expression*

declaration = *type* {$_1$, *name* } :

definition = **PROTOCOL** *name* **IS** *simple.protocol* :
| **PROTOCOL** *name* **IS** *sequential.protocol* :
| **PROTOCOL** *name*
CASE
{ *tagged.protocol* }
:
| **PROC** *name* ({$_0$, *formal* })
procedure.body
:
| {$_1$, *primitive.type* } **FUNCTION** *name* ({$_0$, *formal* })
function.body
:
| {$_1$, *primitive.type* } **FUNCTION** *name* ({$_0$, *formal* }) **IS** *expression.list* :
| *specifier name* **RETYPES** *element* :
| **VAL** *specifier name* **RETYPES** *expression* :

delayed.input = *timer* ? **AFTER** *expression*

digit = 0 | 1 | 2 | 3 | 4 | 5 | 6 | 7 | 8 | 9

element = *element* [*subscript*]
| [*element* **FROM** *subscript* **FOR** *count*]
| *name*

exponent = +*digits* | −*digits*

expression = *monadic.operator operand*
| *operand dyadic.operator operand*
| *conversion*
| *operand*
| **MOSTPOS** *type* | **MOSTNEG** *type*

expression.list = (*value.process*
)
| *name* ({$_0$, *expression* })
| {$_1$, *expression* }

formal = *specifier* {$_1$, *name* }
| **VAL** *specifier* {$_1$, *name* }

function.body = *value.process*

guard   =   *input*
              | *boolean* **&** *input*
              | *boolean* **&** **SKIP**

guarded.alternative   =   *guard*
                                    process

guarded.choice   =   *boolean*
                               process

hex.digit   =   *digit* | **A** | **B** | **C** | **D** | **E** | **F**

input   =   *channel* **?** *variable*
              | *channel* **?** *input.item*
              | *channel* **?** { $_1$ **;** *input.item* }
              | *channel* **?** **CASE** *tagged.list*
              | *timer.input*
              | *delayed.input*
              | *port* **?** *variable*

input.item   =   *variable*
              | *variable* **: :** *variable*

instance   =   *name* **(** { $_0$ **,** *actual* } **)**

integer   =   *digits* | **#** *hex.digits*

literal   =   *integer*
              | *byte*
              | *integer* (*type*)
              | *byte* (*type*)
              | *real* (*type*)
              | *string*
              | **TRUE** | **FALSE**

loop   =   **WHILE** *boolean*
                  process

operand   =   *element*
              | *literal*
              | *table*
              | (*expression*)
              | (*value.process*
)
              | *name* **(** { $_0$ **,** *expression* } **)**

option   =   { $_1$ **,** *case.expression* }
                       process
              | **ELSE**
                       process
              | *specification*
                    option

output   =   *channel* **!** *expression*
              | *channel* **!** *output.item*
              | *channel* **!** { $_1$ **;** *output.item* }
              | *channel* **!** *tag*
              | *channel* **!** *tag* **;** { $_1$ **;** *output.item* }
              | *port* **!** *expression*

output.item =   *expression*
                  | *expression* : : *expression*

parallel =   **PAR**
                          { *process* }
                  | **PAR** *replicator*
                          process
                  | **PRI PAR**
                          { *process* }
                  | **PRI PAR** *replicator*
                          process
                  | *placedpar*

placedpar =   **PLACED PAR**
                          { *placedpar* }
                  | **PLACED PAR** *replicator*
                          placedpar
                  | **PROCESSOR** *expression*
                          process

port =   *element*

primitive.type =   **CHAN OF** *protocol*
                     | **TIMER**
                     | **BOOL**
                     | **BYTE**
                     | **INT**
                     | **INT16**
                     | **INT32**
                     | **INT64**
                     | **REAL32**
                     | **REAL64**
                     | **PORT OF** *type*

procedure.body =   *process*

process =   **SKIP | STOP**
                  | *action*
                  | *construction*
                  | *instance*
                  | *case.input*
                  | *specification*
                      process
                  | *allocation*
                      process

protocol =   *name*
                  | *simple.protocol*
                  | **ANY**

real =   *digits . digits* | *digits . digits***E***exponent*

replicator =   *name* = *base* **FOR** *count*

selection =   **CASE** *selector*
                      { *option* }

selector =   *expression*

sequence = **SEQ**
                          { *process* }
                    | **SEQ** *replicator*
                              process

sequential.protocol = {₁ ; *simple.protocol* }

simple.protocol = *type*
                            | *primitive.type* : : [ ] *type*

specification = *declaration* | *abbreviation* | *definition*

specifier = *primitive.type*
                    | [ ] *specifier*
                    | [*expression*] *specifier*

subscript = *expression*

table = *table* [*subscript*]
                | [{₁ , *expression* }]
                | [*table* **FROM** *subscript* **FOR** *count*]

tag = *name*

tagged.list = *tag*
                      | *tag* ; {₁ ; *input.item* }

tagged.protocol = *tag*
                          | *tag* ; *sequential.protocol*

timer = *element*

timer.input = *timer* ? *variable*

type = *primitive.type*
              | *array.type*

valof = **VALOF**
                    process
                    RESULT *expression.list*
              | *specification*
                    valof

value.process = *valof*

variable = *element*

variable.list = {₁ , *variable* }

variant = *tagged.list*
                      process
                  | *specification*
                      variant

This section provides a complete list of occam symbols and keywords.

Arithmetic operators		Communication symbols	
+	plus	!	Input
–	minus	?	Output
*	times	**Other symbols**	
/	divide	#	Hexadecimal
\	remainder	&	Ampersand; used in a guard
Bit operators		(	Parentheses; used to delimit expressions,
/\	and	)	the type of literals and a parameter list
\/	or	[	Square brackets; used to delimit array subscripts,
><	exclusive or	]	and to construct segments and tables
~	not	[]	Array type specifier
<<	left shift	::	Counted array communication
>>	right shift	:=	Assignment symbol
Relational operators		"	Double quote; used to construct a string byte table
=	equal	'	Single quote; used to delimit character byte literal
<	less than	,	Separator for specifications, parameters, and table
>	greater than	;	Sequential protocol separator
<=	less than or equal to	:	Specification terminator
>=	greater than or equal to	--	Comment introduction
<>	not equal		

AFTER	later than operator	PAR	parallel
ALT	alternation	PLACE	allocation
AND	boolean and operator	PLACED	placed processes
ANY	anarchic protocol	PLUS	modulo addition operator
AT	at *location*	PORT OF	port type
BITAND	bitwise and operator	PRI	prioritised construction
BITNOT	bitwise not operator	PROC	procedure
BITOR	bitwise or operator	PROCESSOR	processor allocation
BOOL	boolean type	PROTOCOL	protocol definition
BYTE	byte type	REAL32	32bit real type
CASE	selection, variant protocol, case input	REAL64	64bit real type
CHAN OF	channel type	REM	remainder operator
ELSE	default selection	RESULT	value process result
FALSE	boolean constant	RETYPES	retyping conversion
FOR	count	ROUND	rounding operator
FROM	base	SEQ	sequence
FUNCTION	function definition	SIZE	array size operator
IF	conditional	SKIP	skip process
IS	specification introduction	STOP	stop process
INT	integer type	TIMER	timer type
INT16	16bit integer type	TIMES	modulo multiplication operator
INT32	32bit integer type	TRUE	boolean constant
INT64	64bit integer type	TRUNC	truncation operator
MINUS	modulo subtraction/negation operator	VAL	value
MOSTNEG	most negative	VALOF	value process
MOSTPOS	most positive	WHILE	loop
NOT	boolean not operator		
OR	boolean or operator		

If an implementation adds further reserved words, then the names used must not include lower case letters.

Characters in occam are represented according to the American Standard Code for Information Interchange (ASCII). Where the full character set is not available occam guarantees the following subset:

```
ABCDEFGHIJKLMNOPQRSTUVWXYZ
abcdefghijklmnopqrstuvwxyz
0123456789
!"#&'()*+,-./:;<=>?[]
```

For reference, here is a table of all printable ASCII characters, and their values:

ASCII	Dec	Hex	ASCII	Dec	Hex	ASCII	Dec	Hex
SPACE	32	20	@	64	40	`	96	60
!	33	21	A	65	41	a	97	61
"	34	22	B	66	42	b	98	62
#	35	23	C	67	43	c	99	63
$	36	24	D	68	44	d	100	64
%	37	25	E	69	45	e	101	65
&	38	26	F	70	46	f	102	66
'	39	27	G	71	47	g	103	67
(	40	28	H	72	48	h	104	68
)	41	29	I	73	49	i	105	69
*	42	2A	J	74	4A	j	106	6A
+	43	2B	K	75	4B	k	107	6B
,	44	2C	L	76	4C	l	108	6C
-	45	2D	M	77	4D	m	109	6D
.	46	2E	N	78	4E	n	110	6E
/	47	2F	O	79	4F	o	111	6F
0	48	30	P	80	50	p	112	70
1	49	31	Q	81	51	q	113	71
2	50	32	R	82	52	r	114	72
3	51	33	S	83	53	s	115	73
4	52	34	T	84	54	t	116	74
5	53	35	U	85	55	u	117	75
6	54	36	V	86	56	v	118	76
7	55	37	W	87	57	w	119	77
8	56	38	X	88	58	x	120	78
9	57	39	Y	89	59	y	121	79
:	58	3A	Z	90	5A	z	122	7A
;	59	3B	[	91	5B	{	123	7B
<	60	3C	\	92	5C			124	7C
=	61	3D	]	93	5D	}	125	7D
>	62	3E	^	94	5E	~	126	7E
?	63	3F	_	95	5F			

The characters *, ' and " may not be used directly in strings or as character constants. These and non-printable characters (such as carriage return, tab etc..) can be included in strings, or used as character constants, in the following form:

*c	*C	carriage return	= *#0D
*n	*N	newline	= *#0A
*t	*T	tab	= *#08
*s	*S	space	= *#20
*'		quotation mark	
*"		double quotation mark	
**		asterisk	

In addition, any byte value can be represented by ***#** followed by two hexadecimal digits, for example:

soh := '*#01'	'*#01' is a byte constant.

This appendix provides a complete list of the standard library routines. The behaviour of routines is described in detail in the following appendices. Library routines (typically the most primitive routines) may be predefined in an implementation, that is, they may be known to the compiler and do not need to be explicitly referenced by the programmer. Other libraries must be explicitly referenced by the programmer, and the name used in their specification has the same property as any other specification. However, programmers are discouraged from using the names of any library routine for any specification other than that of naming the routine in question. The following tables include the name of the routine, and a specifier which indicates the type of each of the parameters to the routine.

J.1   Multiple length integer arithmetic functions

The arithmetic functions provide arithmetic shifts, word rotations and the primitives to construct multiple length arithmetic and multiple length shift operations.

Result	Function	Parameter specifiers
INT	LONGADD	(VAL INT, VAL INT, VAL INT)
INT	LONGSUB	(VAL INT, VAL INT, VAL INT)
INT	ASHIFTRIGHT	(VAL INT, VAL INT)
INT	ASHIFTLEFT	(VAL INT, VAL INT)
INT	ROTATERIGHT	(VAL INT, VAL INT)
INT	ROTATELEFT	(VAL INT, VAL INT)
INT, INT	LONGSUM	(VAL INT, VAL INT, VAL INT)
INT, INT	LONDIFF	(VAL INT, VAL INT, VAL INT)
INT, INT	LONGPROD	(VAL INT, VAL INT, VAL INT)
INT, INT	LONGDIV	(VAL INT, VAL INT, VAL INT)
INT, INT	SHIFTLEFT	(VAL INT, VAL INT, VAL INT)
INT, INT	SHIFTRIGHT	(VAL INT, VAL INT, VAL INT)
INT, INT, INT	NORMALISE	(VAL INT, VAL INT)

J.2   Floating point functions

The floating point functions provide the list of facilities suggested by the ANSI/IEEE standard 754-1985.

Result	Function	Parameter specifiers
REAL32	ABS	(VAL REAL32)
REAL64	DABS	(VAL REAL64)
REAL32	SCALEB	(VAL REAL32, VAL INT)
REAL64	DSCALEB	(VAL REAL64, VAL INT)
REAL32	COPYSIGN	(VAL REAL32, VAL REAL32)
REAL64	DCOPYSIGN	(VAL REAL64, VAL REAL64)
REAL32	SQRT	(VAL REAL32)
REAL64	DSQRT	(VAL REAL64)
REAL32	MINUSX	(VAL REAL32)
REAL64	DMINUSX	(VAL REAL64)
REAL32	NEXTAFTER	(VAL REAL32, VAL REAL32)
REAL64	DNEXTAFTER	(VAL REAL64, VAL REAL64)

Result	Function	Parameter specifiers
REAL32	MULBY2	(VAL REAL32)
REAL64	DMULBY2	(VAL REAL64)
REAL32	DIVBY2	(VAL REAL32)
REAL64	DDIVBY2	(VAL REAL64)
REAL32	LOGB	(VAL REAL32)
REAL64	DLOGB	(VAL REAL64)
BOOL	ISNAN	(VAL REAL32)
BOOL	DISNAN	(VAL REAL64)
BOOL	NOTFINITE	(VAL REAL32)
BOOL	DNOTFINITE	(VAL REAL64)
BOOL	ORDERED	(VAL REAL32,VAL REAL32)
BOOL	DORDERED	(VAL REAL64,VAL REAL64)
INT,REAL32	FLOATING.UNPACK	(VAL REAL32)
INT,REAL64	DFLOATING.UNPACK	(VAL REAL64)
BOOL,INT32,REAL32	ARGUMENT.REDUCE	(VAL REAL32,VAL REAL32,VAL REAL32)
BOOL,INT32,REAL64	DARGUMENT.REDUCE	(VAL REAL64,VAL REAL64,VAL REAL64)
REAL32	FPINT	(VAL REAL32)
REAL64	DFPINT	(VAL REAL64)

J.3   Full IEEE arithmetic functions

Result	Function	Parameter specifiers
REAL32	REAL32OP	(VAL REAL32,VAL INT,VAL REAL32)
REAL64	REAL64OP	(VAL REAL64,VAL INT,VAL REAL64)
BOOL, REAL32	IEEE32OP	(VAL REAL32,VAL INT,VAL INT,VAL REAL32)
BOOL, REAL64	IEEE64OP	(VAL REAL64,VAL INT,VAL INT,VAL REAL64)
REAL32	REAL32REM	(VAL REAL32,VAL REAL32)
REAL64	REAL64REM	(VAL REAL64,VAL REAL64)
BOOL, REAL32	IEEE32REM	(VAL REAL32,VAL REAL32)
BOOL, REAL64	IEEE64REM	(VAL REAL64,VAL REAL64)
BOOL	REAL32EQ	(VAL REAL32,VAL REAL32)
BOOL	REAL64EQ	(VAL REAL64,VAL REAL64)
BOOL	REAL32GT	(VAL REAL32,VAL REAL32)
BOOL	REAL64GT	(VAL REAL64,VAL REAL64)
INT	IEEECOMPARE	(VAL REAL32,VAL REAL32)
INT	DIEEECOMPARE	(VAL REAL64,VAL REAL64)

J.4   Elementary function library

All the functions which begin with the letter D return a value of type **REAL64**, with the exception of **DRAN** which returns an **INT64** value. All other functions return a value of type **REAL32**, with the exception of **RAN** which returns a value of type **INT32**

Result		Function	Parameter specifiers
REAL32		ALOG	(VAL REAL32)
REAL64		DALOG	(VAL REAL64)
REAL32		ALOG10	(VAL REAL32)
REAL64		DALOG10	(VAL REAL64)
REAL32		EXP	(VAL REAL32)
REAL64		DEXP	(VAL REAL64)
REAL32		TAN	(VAL REAL32)
REAL64		DTAN	(VAL REAL64)
REAL32		SIN	(VAL REAL32)
REAL64		DSIN	(VAL REAL64)
REAL32		ASIN	(VAL REAL32)
REAL64		DASIN	(VAL REAL64)
REAL32		COS	(VAL REAL32)
REAL64		DCOS	(VAL REAL64)
REAL32		ACOS	(VAL REAL32)
REAL64		DACOS	(VAL REAL64)
REAL32		SINH	(VAL REAL32)
REAL64		DSINH	(VAL REAL64)
REAL32		COSH	(VAL REAL32)
REAL64		DCOSH	(VAL REAL64)
REAL32		TANH	(VAL REAL32)
REAL64		DTANH	(VAL REAL64)
REAL32		ATAN	(VAL REAL32)
REAL64		DATAN	(VAL REAL64)
REAL32		ATAN2	(VAL REAL32, VAL REAL32)
REAL64		DATAN2	(VAL REAL64, VAL REAL64)
REAL32,	INT32	RAN	(VAL INT32)
REAL64,	INT64	DRAN	(VAL INT64)
REAL32		POWER	(VAL REAL32, VAL REAL32)
REAL64		DPOWER	(VAL REAL64, VAL REAL64)

J.5   Value, string conversion procedures

The library provides primitive procedures to convert a value to and from decimal or hexadecimal representations.

Procedure	Parameter specifiers
`INTTOSTRING`	`(INT, []BYTE, VAL INT)`
`INT16TOSTRING`	`(INT, []BYTE, VAL INT16)`
`INT32TOSTRING`	`(INT, []BYTE, VAL INT32)`
`INT64TOSTRING`	`(INT, []BYTE, VAL INT64)`
`STRINGTOINT`	`(BOOL, INT, VAL []BYTE)`
`STRINGTOINT16`	`(BOOL, INT16, VAL []BYTE)`
`STRINGTOINT32`	`(BOOL, INT32, VAL []BYTE)`
`STRINGTOINT64`	`(BOOL, INT64, VAL []BYTE)`
`HEXTOSTRING`	`(INT, []BYTE, VAL INT)`
`HEX16TOSTRING`	`(INT, []BYTE, VAL INT16)`
`HEX32TOSTRING`	`(INT, []BYTE, VAL INT32)`
`HEX64TOSTRING`	`(INT, []BYTE, VAL INT64)`
`STRINGTOHEX`	`(BOOL, INT, VAL []BYTE)`
`STRINGTOHEX16`	`(BOOL, INT16, VAL []BYTE)`
`STRINGTOHEX32`	`(BOOL, INT32, VAL []BYTE)`
`STRINGTOHEX64`	`(BOOL, INT64, VAL []BYTE)`
`STRINGTOREAL32`	`(BOOL, REAL32, VAL []BYTE)`
`STRINGTOREAL64`	`(BOOL, REAL64, VAL []BYTE)`
`REAL32TOSTRING`	`(INT, []BYTE, VAL REAL32, VAL INT)`
`REAL64TOSTRING`	`(INT, []BYTE, VAL REAL64, VAL INT)`
`STRINGTOBOOL`	`(BOOL, BOOL, VAL []BYTE)`
`BOOLTOSTRING`	`(INT, []BYTE, VAL BOOL)`

The floating point functions described in this appendix provide the list of facilities suggested by the ANSI/IEEE standard 754-1985.

Each function is specified by a skeletal function declaration, a predicate stating the relationship between the actual parameters after the function call and an informal textual description of the operation. All functions are implemented in a way which allows the same variable to be used as both the input and receiving variable in an assignment. The predicate gives the formal definition of the operation, although for most purposes the text will be an adequate explanation.

NaN and *Inf* are the sets of all Not-a-Numbers and all infinities in the format.

K.1   Not-a-number values

Floating point arithmetic implementations will return the following valued Not-a-Numbers to signify the various errors that can occur in evaluations.

Error	Single length value	Double length value
Divide zero by zero	#7FC00000	#7FF80000 00000000
Divide infinity by infinity	#7FA00000	#7FF40000 00000000
Multiply zero by infinity	#7F900000	#7FF20000 00000000
Addition of opposite signed infinities	#7F880000	#7FF10000 00000000
Subtraction of same signed infinities	#7F880000	#7FF10000 00000000
Negative square root	#7F840000	#7FF08000 00000000
REAL64 to **REAL32** NaN conversion	#7F820000	#7FF04000 00000000
Remainder from infinity	#7F804000	#7FF00800 00000000
Remainder by zero	#7F802000	#7FF00400 00000000

K.2   Absolute

```
REAL32 FUNCTION ABS (VAL REAL32 X)
  ...
:
REAL64 FUNCTION DABS (VAL REAL64 X)
  ...
:
```

$ABS(X) = |X|$

This returns the absolute value of **X**. This is implemented clearing the sign bit so that -0.0 becomes $+0.0$ and even though Not-a-Numbers (NaNs) have no signed-ness the sign bit in their representation will be cleared.

K.3   Square root

```
REAL32 FUNCTION SQRT (VAL REAL32 X)
  ...
:
REAL64 FUNCTION DSQRT (VAL REAL64 X)
  ...
:
```

$SQRT\ (X) = \sqrt{X}.$

This returns the square root of **X**. Negative arguments produce a Negative square root Not-a-Number, and infinity produces an infinity.

K.4   Test for Not-a-Number

```
BOOL FUNCTION ISNAN (VAL REAL32 X)
  ...
:
BOOL FUNCTION DISNAN (VAL REAL64 X)
  ...
:
```

$ISNAN(X) = TRUE \Leftrightarrow X \in NaN$

This returns **TRUE** if **X** is a Not-a-Number and **FALSE** otherwise.

K.5   Test for Not-a-Number or infinity

```
BOOL FUNCTION NOTFINITE (VAL REAL32 X)
  ...
:
BOOL FUNCTION DNOTFINITE (VAL REAL64 X)
  ...
:
```

$NOTFINITE(X) = TRUE \Leftrightarrow X \in NaN \cup Inf$

This returns **TRUE** if **X** is a Not-a-Number or an infinity and **FALSE** otherwise.

K.6   Scale by power of two

```
REAL32 FUNCTION SCALEB (VAL REAL32 X, VAL INT n)
  ...
:
REAL64 FUNCTION DSCALEB (VAL REAL64 X, VAL INT n)
  ...
:
```

$$\text{SCALEB}(\mathbf{X}, n) = \mathbf{X} \times 2^n$$

This multiplies **X** by 2^n. Overflow and underflow behaviour is as for normal multiplication under the ANSI/IEEE standard 754-1985. **n** can take any value as the operation will return the correct result even when 2^n cannot be represented in the format.

K.7   Return exponent

```
REAL32 FUNCTION LOGB (VAL REAL32 X)
  ...
:
REAL64 FUNCTION DLOGB (VAL REAL64 X)
  ...
:
```

$\text{LOGB } (\mathbf{X}) = $ result

where $\mathbf{X} \notin Inf \cup NaN \wedge \mathbf{X} \neq 0 \Rightarrow result = \textbf{REAL32}(\mathbf{X.exp} - Bias)$
$\mathbf{X} = 0 \Rightarrow result = -inf$
$\mathbf{X} \in Inf \Rightarrow result = +inf$
$\mathbf{X} \in NaN \Rightarrow result = \mathbf{X}$

This returns the exponent of **X** as an integer valued floating point number; special cases for Infs, NaNs and zero. **NOTE** that all denormalised numbers return the same value – this is not equivalent to rounding the logarithm to an integer value. If **X** is a NaN then it is returned as the result, if **X** is an infinity then the result is plus infinity and if **X** is zero then the result is minus infinity.

K.8   Unpack floating point value

```
INT, REAL32 FUNCTION FLOATING.UNPACK (VAL REAL32 X)
  ...
:
INT, REAL64 FUNCTION DFLOATING.UNPACK (VAL REAL64 X)
  ...
:
```

$\text{FLOATING.UNPACK } (\mathbf{X}) = $ (n, r)

where $\mathbf{X} = 0 \vee \mathbf{X} \in Inf \cup NaN \Rightarrow r \in NaN \wedge n = RealExp - Bias$
"otherwise" $\mathbf{X} = r \times 2^n \wedge r \in [1, 2)$

This "unpacks" **X** into a real (*r*) and an integer (*n*) so that *r* lies between 1 and 2 and that $\mathbf{X} = r \times 2^n$. This is useful for reducing a value to the primary range for "exponential" type functions. If **X** is an infinity or a NaN then a NaN is returned in *r* and *n* holds MaxExp - the exponent of a NaN. If **X** is zero then a NaN is returned in *r* and MaxExp in *n* - this is because the methods used to evaluate a function in its primary range will not be defined for **0.0** which should have already been dealt with as a special case. The use of a NaN in these cases signals an error in the attempt to produce a "primary range" value and offset from **X**.

K.9   Negate

```
REAL32 FUNCTION MINUSX (VAL REAL32 X)
  . . .
:
REAL64 FUNCTION DMINUSX (VAL REAL64 X)
  . . .
:
```

MINUSX (X) =   result
                 where $result.sign = toggle\mathbf{X}.sign, result.frac = \mathbf{X}.frac, result.exp = \mathbf{X}.exp$

This returns **X** with the sign bit toggled. This is not the same as (0 − **X**) as it has different behaviour on zero and NaNs. This should not be used as a unary negation where (0 − **X**) should be used. As with **ABS** it does affect the representation of NaNs even though they have no sign in their interpretation.

K.10   Copy sign

```
REAL32 FUNCTION COPYSIGN (VAL REAL32 X, Y)
  . . .
:
REAL64 FUNCTION DCOPYSIGN (VAL REAL64 X, Y)
  . . .
:
```

COPYSIGN (X, Y) =   result
                      where $result.sign = \mathbf{Y}.sign, result.frac = \mathbf{X}.frac, result.exp = \mathbf{X}.exp$

This returns **X** with the sign bit from **Y**.

K.11   Next representable value

```
REAL32 FUNCTION NEXTAFTER (VAL REAL32 X, Y)
  . . .
:
REAL64 FUNCTION DNEXTAFTER (VAL REAL64 X, Y)
  . . .
:
```

NEXTAFTER (X, Y) =   result
                       where $\mathbf{X} \in NaN \vee \mathbf{Y} \in NaN \Rightarrow result \in NaN \cap \{X, Y\}$
                                $\mathbf{X} = \mathbf{Y} \Rightarrow \mathbf{X}$
                                $\mathbf{X} \neq \mathbf{Y} \Rightarrow$ "result is next real after **X** in the direction of **Y**"

This can be specified precisely but as several subsidiary definitions are required first the informal third line of the "predicate" is used for brevity.

This returns the first floating point number from **X** in the direction of **Y**. The major area where this will be used is in interval arithmetic. If either or both of **X** or **Y** is a NaN then a NaN equal to **X** or **Y** is returned. An overflow from a finite **X** to an infinite result is handled in the same way as an arithmetic overflow.

K.12   Test for orderability

```
BOOL FUNCTION ORDERED (VAL REAL32 X,Y)
  ...
:
BOOL FUNCTION DORDERED (VAL REAL64 X,Y)
  ...
:
```

ORDERED(X, Y) = **TRUE** $\Leftrightarrow$ **X** $\notin NaN \wedge$ **Y** $\notin NaN$

This returns **TRUE** if **X** and **Y** are "orderable" as defined by the ANSI/IEEE standard 754-1985. This implements the negation of the *unordered* comparison in ANSI/IEEE 754-1985 §5.7 and enables the full IEEE style comparison to be derived from the standard <, >, ... comparisons of real types in occam.

K.13   Perform range reduction

```
BOOL,INT32,REAL32 FUNCTION ARGUMENT.REDUCE (VAL REAL32 X, Y, Y.err)
  ...
:
BOOL,INT32,REAL64 FUNCTION DARGUMENT.REDUCE (VAL REAL64 X, Y, Y.err)
  ...
:
```

ARGUMENT.REDUCE$(X, Y, \mathbf{error})$ = (b, n, r)

$$\begin{aligned}
\textit{where}\quad &X.exp \leq Y.exp + maxexpdiff \Rightarrow\; b \wedge X = n \times (Y + \mathbf{error}) + r\\
&\qquad\qquad \wedge (r < (Y + \mathbf{error})/2 \vee (r = (Y + \mathbf{error})/2 \wedge n\, MOD\, 2 = 0))\\
&X.exp > Y.exp + maxexpdiff \Rightarrow\; \exists m : \mathbf{Z}\\
&\qquad\qquad \neg b \wedge X = m \times Y + r\\
&\qquad\qquad \wedge (r < Y/2 \vee (r = Y/2 \wedge m\, MOD\, 2 = 0))\\
&\qquad\qquad \wedge n = undefined
\end{aligned}$$

where $maxexpdiff$ is 20 for **ARGUMENT.REDUCE** and 30 for **DARGUMENT.REDUCE**.

This performs a more accurate remainder **X REM Y** by using an extended precision value for **Y** where possible. It is assumed that **error** is no larger than a last bit error in **Y**. **TRUE** is returned as the boolean result b to indicate that the more accurate remainder has been done and the integer result n will then be the quotient. If the more accurate remainder cannot be done a normal remainder is performed and the quotient n must be calculated separately. This is designed to be used to reduce an argument to the primary range for cyclical functions - such as the trigonometric functions.

K.14   Fast multiply by two

```
REAL32 FUNCTION MULBY2 (VAL REAL32 X)
  ...
:
REAL64 FUNCTION DMULBY2 (VAL REAL64 X)
  ...
:
```

MULBY2(X) = **X** $\times 2$

This returns 2 times **X** with overflow handling as defined in the ANSI/IEEE standard 754-1985.

K.15   Fast divide by two

```
REAL32 FUNCTION DIVBY2 (VAL REAL32 X)
  . . .
:
REAL64 FUNCTION DDIVBY2 (VAL REAL64 X)
  . . .
:
```

$\text{DIVBY2}(X) = X \div 2$

This returns **X** divided by 2 with underflow handling as defined in the ANSI/IEEE standard 754-1985.

K.16   Round to floating point integer

```
REAL32 FUNCTION FPINT (VAL REAL32 X)
  . . .
:
REAL64 FUNCTION DFPINT (VAL REAL64 X)
  . . .
:
```

$$\text{FPINT } (X) = \begin{array}{ll} result \\ where & |X| \geq 2^{bitsperword} \Rightarrow result = X \\ & |X| < 2^{bitsperword} \Rightarrow result = \text{REAL32 (INT ROUND X)} \end{array}$$

This returns **X** rounded to a floating point integer value.

The following arithmetic functions provide arithmetic shifts, word rotations and the primitives to construct multiple length integer arithmetic and multiple length shift operations.

LONGADD	signed addition with a carry in.
LONGSUM	unsigned addition with a carry in and a carry out.
LONGSUB	signed subtraction with a borrow in.
LONGDIFF	unsigned subtraction with a borrow in and a borrow out.
LONGPROD	unsigned multiplication with a carry in, producing a double length result.
LONGDIV	unsigned division of a double length number, producing a single length result.
SHIFTRIGHT	right shift on a double length quantity.
SHIFTLEFT	left shift on a double length quantity.
NORMALISE	normalise a double length quantity.
ASHIFTRIGHT	arithmetic right shift on a double length quantity.
ASHIFTLEFT	arithmetic left shift on a double length quantity.
ROTATERIGHT	rotate a word right.
ROTATELEFT	rotate a word left.

For the purpose of explanation imagine a new type *INTEGER*, and the associated conversion. This imaginary type is capable of representing the complete set of integers and is presumed to be represented as an infinite bit two's complement number. With this one exception the following are occam descriptions of the various arithmetic functions.

```
-- constants used in the following description
VAL bitsperword  IS machine.wordsize(INTEGER) :
VAL range        IS storeable.values(INTEGER) :
                 -- range = 2^{bitsperword}
VAL maxint       IS INTEGER (MOSTPOS INT) :
                 -- maxint = (range/2 - 1)
VAL minint       IS INTEGER (MOSTNEG INT) :
                 -- minint = -(range/2)
-- INTEGER literals
VAL one          IS 1(INTEGER) :
VAL two          IS 2(INTEGER) :
-- mask
VAL wordmask     IS range - one :
```

In occam, values are considered to be signed. However, in these functions the concern is with other interpretations. In the construction of multiple length arithmetic the need is to interpret words as containing both signed and unsigned integers. In the following the new *INTEGER* type is used to manipulate these values, and other values which may require more than a single word to store.

The sign conversion of a value is defined in the functions **unsign** and **sign**. These are used in the description following but they are NOT functions themselves.

INTEGER **FUNCTION unsign (VAL INT operand)**

    -- Returns the value of **operand** as an unsigned integer value.
    -- for example, on a 32 bit word machine :
    -- **unsign (1)** = 1
    -- **unsign (−1)** = $2^{32} - 1$

    INTEGER **operand.i**
    VALOF
      IF
        operand < 0
          operand.i := (*INTEGER*** operand) + range**
        operand >= 0
          operand.i := *INTEGER* **operand**
      RESULT operand.i
:

INT FUNCTION sign (VAL *INTEGER* **result.i)**

    -- Takes the *INTEGER* **result.i** and returns the signed type **INT**.
    -- for example, on a 32 bit word machine :
    -- $2^{31} - 1$ becomes $2^{31} - 1$
    -- 2^{31} becomes -2^{31}

    INT result :
    VALOF
      IF
        (result.i > maxint) AND (result.i < range)
          result := INT (result.i - range)
        TRUE
          result := INT result.i
      RESULT result
:

L.1   The integer arithmetic functions

LONGADD performs the addition of signed quantities with a carry in. The function is invalid if arithmetic overflow occurs.

The action of the function is defined as follows:

```
INT FUNCTION LONGADD (VAL INT left, right, carry.in)

  -- Adds (signed) left word to right word with least significant bit of carry.in.

  INTEGER sum.i, carry.i, left.i, right.i :
  VALOF
    SEQ
      carry.i := INTEGER (carry.in /\ 1)
      left.i  := INTEGER left
      right.i := INTEGER right
      sum.i   := (left.i + right.i) + carry.i
    -- overflow may occur in the following conversion
    -- resulting in an invalid process
    RESULT INT sum.i
:
```

LONGSUM performs the addition of unsigned quantities with a carry in and a carry out. No overflow can occur.

The action of the function is defined as follows:

```
INT, INT FUNCTION LONGSUM (VAL INT left, right, carry.in)

  -- Adds (unsigned) left word to right word with the least significant bit of carry.in.
  -- Returns two results, the first value is one if a carry occurs, zero otherwise,
  -- the second result is the sum.

  INT carry.out :
  INTEGER sum.i, left.i, right.i :
  VALOF
    SEQ
      left.i := unsign (left)
      right.i := unsign (right)
      sum.i := (left.i + right.i) + INTEGER (carry.in /\ 1)
      IF                        -- assign carry
        sum.i >= range
          SEQ
            sum.i := sum.i - range
            carry.out := 1
        TRUE
          carry.out := 0
    RESULT carry.out, sign (sum.i)
:
```

LONGSUB performs the subtraction of signed quantities with a borrow in. The function is invalid if arithmetic overflow occurs.

The action of the function is defined as follows:

```
INT FUNCTION LONGSUB (VAL INT left, right, borrow.in)

  -- Subtracts (signed) right word from left word and subtracts borrow.in from the result.

  INTEGER diff.i, borrow.i, left.i, right.i :
  VALOF
    SEQ
      borrow.i := INTEGER (borrow.in /\ 1)
      left.i   := INTEGER left
      right.i  := INTEGER right
      diff.i   := (left.i - right.i) - borrow.i
      -- overflow may occur in the following conversion
      -- resulting in an invalid process
      RESULT INT diff.i
  :
```

LONGDIFF performs the subtraction of unsigned quantities with borrow in and borrow out. No overflow can occur.

The action of the function is defined as follows:

```
INT, INT FUNCTION LONGDIFF (VAL INT left, right, borrow.in)

  -- Subtracts (unsigned) right word from left word and subtracts borrow.in from the result.
  -- Returns two results, the first is one if a borrow occurs, zero otherwise,
  -- the second result is the difference.

  INTEGER diff.i, left.i, right.i :
  VALOF
    SEQ
      left.i := unsign (left)
      right.i := unsign (right)
      diff.i := (left.i - right.i) - INTEGER (borrow.in /\ 1)
      IF      -- assign borrow
        diff.i < 0
          SEQ
            diff.i := diff.i + range
            borrow.out := 1
        TRUE
          borrow.out := 0
      RESULT borrow.out, sign (diff.i)
  :
```

LONGPROD performs the multiplication of two unsigned quantities, adding in an unsigned carry word. Produces a double length unsigned result. No overflow can occur.

The action of the function is defined as follows:

```
INT, INT FUNCTION LONGPROD (VAL INT left, right, carry.in)

  -- Multiplies (unsigned) left word by right word and adds carry.in.
  -- Returns the result as two integers most significant word first.

  INTEGER prod.i, prod.lo.i, prod.hi.i, left.i, right.i, carry.i :
  VALOF
    SEQ
      carry.i := unsign (carry.in)
      left.i  := unsign (left)
      right.i := unsign (right)
      prod.i   := (left.i * right.i) + carry.i
      prod.lo.i := prod.i REM range
      prod.hi.i := prod.i / range
    RESULT sign (prod.hi.i), sign (prod.lo.i)

  :
```

LONGDIV divides an unsigned double length number by an unsigned single length number. The function produces an unsigned single length quotient and an unsigned single length remainder. An overflow will occur if the quotient is not representable as an unsigned single length number. The function becomes invalid if the divisor is equal to zero.

The action of the function is defined as follows:

```
INT, INT FUNCTION LONGDIV (VAL INT dividend.hi, dividend.lo, divisor)

  -- Divides (unsigned) dividend.hi and dividend.lo by divisor.
  -- Returns two results the first is the quotient and the second is the remainder.

  INTEGER divisor.i, dividend.i, hi, lo, quot.i, rem.i :
  VALOF
    SEQ
      hi := unsign (dividend.hi)
      lo := unsign (dividend.lo)
      divisor.i := unsign (divisor)
      dividend.i := (hi * range) + lo
      quot.i := dividend.i / divisor.i
      rem.i  := dividend.i REM divisor.i
    -- overflow may occur in the following conversion of quot.i
    -- resulting in an invalid process
    RESULT sign (quot.i), sign (rem.i)

  :
```

SHIFTRIGHT performs a right shift on a double length quantity. The function must be called with the number of places in range, otherwise the implementation can produce unexpected effects.

i.e. 0 <= **places** <= 2∗**bitsperword**

The action of the function is defined as follows:

```
INT, INT FUNCTION SHIFTRIGHT (VAL INT hi.in, lo.in, places)
```

> -- Shifts the value in **hi.in** and **lo.in** right by the given number of **places**.
> -- Bits shifted in are set to zero.
> -- Returns the result as two integers most significant word first.

```
INT hi.out, lo.out :
VALOF
  IF
    (places < 0) OR (places > (two*bitsperword))
      SEQ
        hi.out := 0
        lo.out := 0
    TRUE
      INTEGER operand, result, hi, lo :
      SEQ
        hi := unsign (hi.in)
        lo := unsign (lo.in)
        operand := (hi << bitsperword) + lo
        result  := operand >> places
        lo := result /\ wordmask
        hi := result >> bitsperword
        hi.out := sign (hi)
        lo.out := sign (lo)
  RESULT hi.out, lo.out
:
```

SHIFTLEFT performs a left shift on a double length quantity. The function must be called with the number of places in range, otherwise the implementation can produce unexpected effects.

i.e. $0 \texttt{<=}$ **places** $\texttt{<=} 2*\texttt{bitsperword}$

The action of the function is defined as follows:

```
INT, INT FUNCTION SHIFTLEFT (VAL INT hi.in, lo.in, places)
```

    -- Shifts the value in **hi.in** and **lo.in** left by the given number of **places**.
    -- Bits shifted in are set to zero.
    -- Returns the result as two integers most significant word first.

```
    VALOF
      IF
        (places < 0) OR (places > (two*bitsperword))
          SEQ
            hi.out := 0
            lo.out := 0
        TRUE
          INTEGER operand, result, hi, lo :
          SEQ
            hi := unsign (hi.in)
            lo := unsign (lo.in)
            operand := (hi << bitsperword) + lo
            result  := operand << places
            lo := result /\ wordmask
            hi := result >> bitsperword
            hi.out := sign (hi)
            lo.out := sign (lo)
      RESULT hi.out, lo.out
:
```

NORMALISE normalises a double length quantity. No overflow can occur.

The action of the function is defined as follows :

```
INT, INT, INT FUNCTION NORMALISE (VAL INT hi.in, lo.in)
```

    -- Shifts the value in `hi.in` and `lo.in` left until the highest bit is set.
    -- The function returns three integer results
    -- The first returns the number of places shifted.
    -- The second and third return the result as two integers with the most significant word first;
    -- If the input value was zero, the first result is 2***bitsperword**.

```
INT places, hi.out, lo.out :
VALOF
  IF
    (hi.in = 0) AND (lo.in = 0)
      places := INT (two*bitsperword)
    TRUE
      VAL msb IS one << ((two*bitsperword) - one) :
      INTEGER operand, hi, lo :
      SEQ
        lo := unsign (lo.in)
        hi := unsign (hi.in)
        operand := (hi << bitsperword) + lo
        places := 0
        WHILE (operand /\ msb) = 0
          SEQ
            operand := operand << one
            places := places + 1
        hi := operand / range
        lo := operand REM range
        hi.out := sign (hi)
        lo.out := sign (lo)
  RESULT places, hi.out, lo.out
:
```

L.2   Arithmetic shifts

ASHIFTRIGHT performs an arithmetic right shift, shifting in and maintaining the sign bit. The function must be called with the number of places in range, otherwise the implementation can produce unexpected effects.

i.e. $0 <=$ **places** $<=$ **bitsperword**

No overflow can occur.

N.B the result of this function is NOT the same as division by a power of two.

  e.g. $-1/2 = 0$
       ASHIFTRIGHT $(-1, 1)$ $= -1$

The action of the function is defined as follows:

  -- Shifts the value in **operand** right by the given number of **places**.
  -- The status of the high bit is maintained

```
INT FUNCTION ASHIFTRIGHT (VAL INT operand, places) IS
                INT( INTEGER(operand) >> places ) :
```

ASHIFTLEFT performs an arithmetic left shift. The function is invalid if significant bits are shifted out, signalling an overflow. The function must be called with the number of places in range, otherwise the implementation can produce unexpected effects.

i.e. $0 <=$ **places** $<=$ **bitsperword**

N.B the result of this function is the same as multiplication by a power of two.

The action of the function is defined as follows:

```
INT FUNCTION ASHIFTLEFT (VAL INT argument, places)

    -- Shifts the value in argument left by the given number of places.
    -- Bits shifted in are set to zero.

    INTEGER result.i :
    VALOF
      result.i := INTEGER(argument) << places
      -- overflow may occur in the following conversion
      -- resulting in an invalid process
      RESULT INT result.i
  :
```

L.3   Word rotation

ROTATERIGHT rotates a word right. Bits shifted out of the word on the right, re-enter the word on the left. The function must be called with the number of places in range, otherwise the implementation can produce unexpected effects.

i.e. 0 <= **places** <= **bitsperword**

No overflow can occur.

The action of the function is defined as follows:

```
INT FUNCTION ROTATERIGHT (VAL INT argument, places)

  -- Rotates the value in argument by the given number of places.

  INTEGER high, low, argument.i :
  VALOF
    SEQ
      argument.i := unsign(argument)
      argument.i := (argument.i * range) >> places
      high := argument.i / range
      low := argument.i REM range
    RESULT INT(high \/ low)
:
```

ROTATELEFT rotates a word left. Bits shifted out of the word on the left, re-enter the word on the right. The function must be called with the number of places in range, otherwise the implementation can produce unexpected effects.

i.e. 0 <= **places** <= **bitsperword**

The action of the function is defined as follows:

```
INT FUNCTION ROTATELEFT (VAL INT argument, places)

  -- Rotates the value in argument by the given number of places.

  INTEGER high, low, argument.i :
  VALOF
    SEQ
      argument.i := unsign(argument)
      argument.i := argument.i << places
      high := argument.i / range
      low := argument.i REM range
    RESULT INT(high \/ low)
:
```

REALOP and **REALREM** are implementations of the ANSI/IEEE 754-1985 floating point arithmetic standard. An implementation should comply to the requirements of the standard in as much as all results returned by them should be correct as defined in the standard. Most programmers will not need to use these functions directly as most occam implementations will compile all real arithmetic as calls to these functions. In some applications, such as interval arithmetic, the rounding modes are needed so the functions will need to be explicitly called in those cases. Also, in some applications, the IEEE standards use of infinities and Not-a-number to handle errors and overflows may be required in preference to the standard occam treatment of them as invalid expressions.

The functions for **REAL32** operands are

```
REAL32 FUNCTION REAL32OP (VAL REAL32 X, VAL INT Op, VAL REAL32 Y)
  ...
:
```

```
REAL32 FUNCTION REAL32REM (VAL REAL32 X, VAL REAL32 Y)
  ...
:
```

REAL32OP (**X, Op, Y**) evaluates $X \ Op \ Y$ according to the standard without error checking, using the conventional rounding mode. The various operations are coded in **Op** where:

```
op   = 0   +
     = 1   -
     = 2   *
     = 3   /
```

REAL32REM (**X, Y**) evaluates $X \ REM \ Y$ according to the standard without error checking.

REAL64OP and **REAL64REM** are defined in an similar manner to operate on **REAL64**s.

IEEExxOP (**X, Rm, Op, Y**) evaluates $X \ Op \ Y$ according to the standard. The rounding mode to be used is indicated by **Rm** where:

```
round_mode   = 0   Round to Zero
round_mode   = 1   Round to Nearest
round_mode   = 2   Round to Plus Infinity
round_mode   = 3   Round to Minus Infinity
```

IEEExxREM (**X, Y**) evaluates $X \ REM \ Y$ according to the standard. The functions are:

```
BOOL, REAL32 FUNCTION IEEE32OP (VAL REAL32 X,
                                VAL INT Rm, Op, VAL REAL32 Y)
  ...
:
BOOL, REAL32 FUNCTION IEEE32REM (VAL REAL32 X, VAL REAL32 Y)
  ...
:
```

These functions return two results, a boolean which is true if an error has occurred, and false otherwise. Where an error has occurred the function will also return the appropriate NaN, otherwise the function returns the result.

IEEE64OP and **IEEE64REM** are defined in a similar manner to operate on **REAL64**s.

M.1   ANSI/IEEE real comparison

The comparisons on the real types provided in the occam language should suffice for most purposes. However, if the comparisons detailed in the ANSI/IEEE 754-1985 standard are required then they can be generated from the set of primitive comparisons.

```
BOOL FUNCTION REAL32EQ (VAL REAL32 X, Y)
  -- result = (X = Y) in the IEEE sense
  ...
:
BOOL FUNCTION REAL32GT (VAL REAL32 X, Y)
  -- result = (X > Y) in the IEEE sense
  ...
:
```

A standard function **IEEECOMPARE** will return a value which indicates which of the relations *less than, greater than, equals* or *unordered* as defined by IEEE 754 paragraph 5.7. This procedure is

```
INT FUNCTION IEEECOMPARE (VAL REAL32 X, Y)
  INT result :
  VALOF
    IF
      ORDERED (X, Y)
        IF
          REAL32EQ (X, Y)
            result := 0
          REAL32GT (X, Y)
            result := 1
          TRUE
            result := -1
      TRUE
        result := 2
    RESULT result
:
```

Then, if really necessary, any of the 26 varieties of comparision suggested by the IEEE standard can be derived. For instance the ? >= predicate could be implemented by

```
        BOOL, BOOL FUNCTION IEEE.UGE. (VAL REAL32 X,Y)
          VAL LT IS -1, EQ IS 0, GT IS 1, UN IS 2:
          INT relation:
          VALOF
            relation := IEEECOMPARE (X, Y)
            RESULT FALSE,
                  (relation=GT) OR ((relation=EQ) OR (relation=UN))
        :
```

Similarily *NOT*(<>) could be implemented as

```
        BOOL, BOOL FUNCTION IEEENOT.LG. (VAL REAL32 X,Y)
          VAL LT IS -1, EQ IS 0, GT IS 1, UN IS 2:
          INT relation:
          VALOF
            relation := IEEECOMPARE (X, Y)
            RESULT (relation=UN), (relation=EQ) OR (relation=UN)
        :
```

In either of these cases the value returned in the first boolean is equivalent to the invalid operation flag being set according to the ANSI/IEEE standard 754-1985.

The double length version **DIEEECOMPARE** is defined in a similar manner to **IEEECOMPARE**.

The elementary function library provides a set of routines which provide elementary functions compatible with the ANSI/IEEE standard 754-1985 for binary floating-point arithmetic.

All single length functions other than **POWER**, **ATAN2** and **RAN** have one parameter which is a **VAL REAL32** taking the argument of the function. **POWER** and **ATAN2** have two parameters. They are both **VAL REAL32s** which receive the arguments of the function. **RAN** has a single parameter which is a **VAL INT32**. In each case the double-length version is obtained by prefixing a **D** onto the function name, whose parameters are **VAL REAL64** or, in the case of **DRAN**, **VAL INT64**.

Accompanying the description of each function is the specification of the function's *Domain* and *Range*. The *Domain* specifies the range of valid inputs, i.e. those for which the output is a normal or denormal floating-point number. The *Range* specifies the range of outputs produced by all arguments in the *Domain*. The given endpoints are not exceeded. Note that some of the domains specified are implementation dependent.

Ranges are given as intervals, using the convention that a square bracket { [or] } means that the adjacent endpoint is included in the range, whilst a round bracket { (or) } means that it is excluded. Endpoints are given to a few significant figures only. Where the range depends on the floating-point format, single-length is indicated with an S and double-length with a D.

For functions with two arguments the complete range of both arguments is given. This means that for each number in one range, there is at least one (though sometimes only one) number in the other range such that the pair of arguments is valid. Both ranges are shown, linked by an 'x'.

In the specifications, XMAX is the largest representable floating-point number: in single-length it is approximately $3.4 * 10^{38}$, and in double-length it is approximately $1.8 * 10^{308}$. Pi means the closest floating-point representation of the transcendental number π, ln(2) the closest representation of $\log_e(2)$, and so on. In describing the algorithm, X is used generically to designate the argument, and "result" to designate the output.

The routines will accept any value, as specified by the IEEE standard, including special values representing **NaNs** ('Not a Number') and **Infs** ('Infinity'). **NaNs** are copied directly to the result, whilst **Infs** may or may not be valid arguments. Valid arguments are those for which the result is a normal (or denormalised) floating-point number.

Arguments outside the domain (apart from **NaNs** which are simply copied to the result) give rise to *exceptional results*, which may be **NaN**, **+Inf**, or **−Inf**. **Infs** mean that the result is mathematically well-defined but too large to be represented in the floating-point format.

Error conditions are reported by means of three distinct **NaNs** :

`undefined.NaN`	This means that the function is mathematically undefined for this argument, for example the logarithm of a negative number.
`unstable.NaN`	This means that a small change in the argument would cause a large change in the value of the function, so any error in the input will render the output meaningless.
`inexact.NaN`	This means that although the mathematical function is well-defined, its value is in range, and it is stable with respect to input errors at this argument, the limitations of word-length (and reasonable cost of the algorithm) make it impossible to compute the correct value.

Implementations will return the following values for these Not-a-Numbers:

Error	Single length value	Double length value
`undefined.NaN`	#7F800010	#7FF00002 00000000
`unstable.NaN`	#7F800008	#7FF00001 00000000
`inexact.NaN`	#7F800004	#7FF00000 80000000

In all cases, the function returns a **NaN** if given a **NaN**.

N.1   Logarithm

```
REAL32 FUNCTION ALOG (VAL REAL32 X)
  . . .
  :
REAL64 FUNCTION DALOG (VAL REAL64 X)
  . . .
  :
```

These compute : result = $\log_e$(**X**).

Domain :   (0, XMAX]
Range :   [MinLog, MaxLog] = $[-103.28, 88.72]S$ = $[-745.2, 709.78]D$

All arguments outside the domain generate an **undefined.NaN**.

N.2   Base 10 logarithm

```
REAL32 FUNCTION ALOG10 (VAL REAL32 X)
  . . .
  :
REAL64 FUNCTION DALOG10 (VAL REAL64 X)
  . . .
  :
```

These compute : result = $\log_{10}$(**X**)

Domain :   (0, XMAX]
Range :   [MinLog10, MaxLog10] = $[-44.85, 38.53]S$ = $[-323.6, 308.25]D$

All arguments outside the domain generate an **undefined.NaN**.

N.3   Exponential

```
REAL32 FUNCTION EXP (VAL REAL32 X)
  . . .
  :
REAL64 FUNCTION DEXP (VAL REAL64 X)
  . . .
  :
```

These compute : result = e^X.

Domain :   [−Inf, MaxLog) = $[-Inf, 88.72)S$, = $[-Inf, 709.78)D$
Range :   [0, XMAX)

If the result is too large to be represented in the floating-point format, **Inf** is returned.

N.4   X to the power of Y

```
REAL32 FUNCTION POWER (VAL REAL32 X, Y)
  . . .
  :
REAL64 FUNCTION DPOWER (VAL REAL64 X, Y)
  . . .
  :
```

These compute : result = X^Y.

Domain :   [0, Inf] x [−Inf, Inf]
Range :   [−Inf, Inf]

If the result is too large to be represented in the floating-point format, **Inf** is returned. If X or Y is **NaN**, **NaN** is returned. Other special cases are as follows :

First Input (X)	Second Input (Y)	Result
$X < 0$	any	undefined.NaN
0	≤ 0	undefined.NaN
0	$0 < Y \leq$ XMAX	0
0	Inf	unstable.NaN
$0 < X < 1$	Inf	0
$0 < X < 1$	−Inf	Inf
1	$-$XMAX $\leq Y \leq$ XMAX	1
1	$\pm$ Inf	unstable.NaN
$1 < X \leq$ XMAX	Inf	Inf
$1 < X \leq$ XMAX	−Inf	0
Inf	$1 \leq Y \leq$ Inf	Inf
Inf	$-$Inf$\leq Y \leq -1$	0
Inf	$-1 < Y < 1$	undefined.NaN
otherwise	0	1
otherwise	1	X

N.5   Sine

```
REAL32 FUNCTION SIN (VAL REAL32 X)
  . . .
:
REAL64 FUNCTION DSIN (VAL REAL64 X)
  . . .
:
```

These compute : result = sine(X)   (where X is in radians).

Domain :   [−Smax, Smax]   = [−12868.0, 12868.0]S, = [−2.1 ∗ 10^8, 2.1 ∗ 10^8]D
Range :   [−1.0, 1.0]

All arguments outside the domain generate an **inexact.NaN**. Implementations may provide a larger domain.

N.6   Cosine

```
REAL32 FUNCTION COS (VAL REAL32 X)
  . . .
:
REAL64 FUNCTION DCOS (VAL REAL64 X)
  . . .
:
```

These compute : result = cosine(X)   (where X is in radians).

Domain :   [−Smax, Smax] = [−12868.0, 12868.0]S, = [−2.1 ∗ 10^8, 2.1 ∗ 10^8]D
Range :   [−1.0, 1.0]

All arguments outside the domain generate an **inexact.NaN**. Implementations may provide a larger domain.

N.7   Tangent

```
REAL32 FUNCTION TAN (VAL REAL32 X)
    . . .
  :
REAL64 FUNCTION DTAN (VAL REAL64 X)
    . . .
  :
```

These compute : result = tan(X)   (where X is in radians).

Domain : $[-\text{Tmax, Tmax}] = [-6434.0, 6434.0]S, = [-1.05 * 10^8, 1.05 * 10^8]D$
Range : $(-\text{Inf, Inf})$

All arguments outside the domain generate an **inexact.NaN**. Implementations may provide a larger domain.

N.8   Arcsine

```
REAL32 FUNCTION ASIN (VAL REAL32 X)
    . . .
  :
REAL64 FUNCTION DASIN (VAL REAL64 X)
    . . .
  :
```

These compute : result = $\text{sine}^{-1}(X)$ (in radians).

Domain : $[-1.0, 1.0]$
Range : $[-\text{Pi/2, Pi/2}]$

All arguments outside the domain generate an **undefined.NaN**.

N.9   Arccosine

```
REAL32 FUNCTION ACOS (VAL REAL32 X)
    . . .
  :
REAL64 FUNCTION DACOS (VAL REAL64 X)
    . . .
  :
```

These compute : result = $\text{cosine}^{-1}(X)$ (in radians).

Domain : $[-1.0, 1.0]$
Range : $[0, \text{Pi}]$

All arguments outside the domain generate an **undefined.NaN**.

N.10   Arctangent

```
REAL32 FUNCTION ATAN (VAL REAL32 X)
  ...
:
REAL64 FUNCTION DATAN (VAL REAL64 X)
  ...
:
```

These compute : result = $\tan^{-1}(X)$ (in radians).

Domain :   [−Inf, Inf]
Range :   [−Pi/2, Pi/2]

N.11   Polar Angle

```
REAL32 FUNCTION ATAN2 (VAL REAL32 X, Y)
  ...
:
REAL64 FUNCTION DATAN2 (VAL REAL64 X, Y)
  ...
:
```

These compute the angular co-ordinate $\tan^{-1}(Y/X)$ (in radians) of a point whose X and Y co-ordinates are given.

Domain :   [−Inf, Inf] x [−Inf, Inf]
Range :   (−Pi, Pi]

(0, 0) and (±**Inf**,±**Inf**) give **undefined.NaN**.

N.12   Hyperbolic sine

```
REAL32 FUNCTION SINH (VAL REAL32 X)
  ...
:
REAL64 FUNCTION DSINH (VAL REAL64 X)
  ...
:
```

These compute : result = sinh(X).

Domain :   [−Hmax, Hmax] $= [−89.4, 89.4]S, = [−710.5, 710.5]D$
Range :   (−Inf, Inf)

$X < -$Hmax gives −**Inf**, and $X >$ Hmax gives **Inf**.

N.13   Hyperbolic cosine

```
REAL32 FUNCTION COSH (VAL REAL32 X)
  ...
:
REAL64 FUNCTION DCOSH (VAL REAL64 X)
  ...
:
```

These compute: result = cosh(X).

Domain : $[-\text{Hmax, Hmax}] = [-89.4, 89.4]S, = [-710.5, 710.5]D$
Range :   [1.0, Inf)

$|X| >$ Hmax gives **Inf**.

N.14   Hyperbolic tangent

```
REAL32 FUNCTION TANH (VAL REAL32 X)
   . . .
:
REAL64 FUNCTION DTANH (VAL REAL64 X)
   . . .
:
```

These compute : result = tanh(X).

Domain :   [−Inf, Inf]
Range :   [−1.0, 1.0]

N.15   Pseudo-random numbers

```
REAL32, INT32 FUNCTION RAN (VAL INT32 N)
   . . .
:
REAL64, INT64 FUNCTION DRAN (VAL INT64 N)
   . . .
:
```

This function returns two results, the first is a real between 0.0 and 1.0, and the second is an integer. The integer, which must be used as the parameter in the next call to the function, carries a pseudo-random linear congruential sequence N_k, and must be kept in scope for as long as the function is used. It should be initialised before the first call to the function but not modified thereafter except by the function itself. Consider the following sequence:

```
SEQ
   x, seed := RAN (8)       -- initialise seed
   y, seed := RAN (seed)
   z, seed := RAN (seed)
```

In this example **x**, **y**, and **z** are each assigned a psuedo- random value.

Domain :   Integers
Range :   [0.0, 1.0) x Integers

This appendix describes the standard library of string to value, value to string routines. The library provides primitive procedures to convert a value to and from decimal or hexadecimal representations. High input/output routines can be easily built using these simple procedures, and a number will typically be provided in an implementation.

O.1   Integer, string conversions

The procedures described here provide conversion between integer values and their decimal or hexadecimal representations held as a string of characters, for example:

```
PROC INTTOSTRING (INT len, []BYTE string, VAL INT n)
  . . .
:
```

The procedure **INTTOSTRING** returns the decimal representation of **n** in **string** and the number of characters in the representation in **len**.

```
PROC STRINGTOINT (BOOL error, INT n, VAL []BYTE string)
  . . .
:
```

The procedure **STRINGTOINT** returns in **n** the value represented by **string**. **error** is set to **TRUE** if a non numeric character is found in **string**. + or a – are allowed in the first character position. **n** will be the value of the the portion of **string** up to any illegal character with the convention that the value of an empty string is 0. **error** is also set if the value of **string** overflows the range of **INT**, in this case **n** will contain the low order bits of the binary representation of **string**. **error** is set to **FALSE** in all other cases.

```
PROC HEXTOSTRING (INT len, []BYTE string, VAL INT n)
  . . .
:
```

The procedure **HEXTOSTRING** returns the hexadecimal representation of **n** in **string** and the number of characters in the representation in **len**. All the nibbles (a nibble is a word 4 bits wide) of **n** are output so that leading zeros are included. The number of characters will be the number of bits in an **INT** divided by 4.

```
PROC STRINGTOHEX (BOOL error, INT n, VAL []BYTE string)
  . . .
:
```

The procedure **STRINGTOHEX** returns in **n** the value represented by the hexadecimal **string**. **error** is set to **TRUE** if a non hexadecimal character is found in **string**. Here **n** will be the value of the the portion of **string** up to the illegal character with the convention that the value of an empty string is 0. **error** is also set to **TRUE** if the value represented by **string** overflows the range of **INT**. In this case **n** will contain the low order bits of the binary representation of **string**. In all other cases **error** is set to **FALSE**.

Similar procedures are provided for the types **INT16**, **INT32** and **INT64**. These procedures use equivalent parameters of the appropriate type. The procedures are:

INTTOSTRING	INT16TOSTRING	INT32TOSTRING	INT64TOSTRING
STRINGTOINT	STRINGTOINT16	STRINGTOINT32	STRINGTOINT64
HEXTOSTRING	HEX16TOSTRING	HEX32TOSTRING	HEX64TOSTRING
STRINGTOHEX	STRINGTOHEX16	STRINGTOHEX32	STRINGTOHEX64

O.2   Boolean, string conversion

The procedures described here provide conversion between boolean values and their textual representation "**TRUE**" and "**FALSE**".

```
PROC BOOLTOSTRING (INT len, []BYTE string, VAL BOOL b)
  . . .
:
```

The procedure **BOOLTOSTRING** returns "**TRUE**" in **string** if **b** is **TRUE** and "**FALSE**" otherwise. **len** contains the number of characters in the string returned.

```
PROC STRINGTOBOOL (BOOL error, b, VAL []BYTE string)
  . . .
:
```

The procedure **STRINGTOBOOL** returns **TRUE** in b if first 4 characters of **string** are "**TRUE**", **FALSE** if first 5 characters are "**FALSE**" and **b** is undefined in other cases. **TRUE** is returned in **error** if **string** is not exactly "**TRUE**" or "**FALSE**".

O.3   Real, string conversion

The procedures described here provide conversion between real values and their representation as strings, for example:

```
PROC STRINGTOREAL32 (BOOL error, REAL32 r, VAL []BYTE string)
  . . .
:
PROC STRINGTOREAL64 (BOOL error, REAL64 r, VAL []BYTE string)
  . . .
:
```

These two procedures each take a string containing a decimal representation of a real number and convert it into the corresponding real value. If the value represented by **string** overflows the range of the type then an appropriately signed infinity is returned. Errors in the syntax of **string** are signalled by a Not-a-Number being returned and **error** being set to **TRUE**. The string is scanned from the left as far as possible while the syntax is still valid. If there any characters after the end of the longest correct string then error is set to **TRUE**, otherwise it is **FALSE**. For example if **string** was "**12.34E+2+1.0**" then the value returned would be 12.34×10^2 with **error** set to **TRUE**. Strings which represent real values are those specified by the syntax for *real* literals, for example:

```
12.34
587.0E-20
+1.0E+123
-3.05
```

Further examples are given in the section on literals on page 25.

```
PROC REAL32TOSTRING (INT len, []BYTE string,
                     VAL REAL32 r, VAL INT m,n)
  . . .
:
PROC REAL64TOSTRING (INT len, []BYTE string,
                     VAL REAL64 r, VAL INT m,n)
  . . .
:
```

These two procedures return a string representing the value **r** in the first **len BYTEs** of **string**. The format of the representation is determined by **m** and **n**. Free format is selected by passing **0** in **m** and **n** into the procedure. Where possible a fixed point representation is used when this does not indicate more accuracy than is available and does not have more than 3 "0"s after the decimal point before significant digits. Otherwise exponential form is used. The number of characters returned in **string** here depends on the input but will be no more than 15 in **REALTOSTRING32** and 24 in **REALTOSTRING64**. **string** is left justified in free format.

If **m** is non-zero then if possible the procedure returns a fixed point representation of **r** with **m** digits before the decimal point and **n** places after with padding spaces being added when needed. If this is not possible then an exponential representation is returned with the same field width as the fixed point representation would have had. If **m** and **n** are both very small then an exponential representation may not fit in the field width so two special values "**Un**" and "**Ov**" with a sign are returned to indicate a value under or over the representable fixed point values. In all these cases **string** is padded with spaces so that it contains (**m** + **n** + 2) characters - **m** before the decimal point, **n** after, as well as the sign and decimal point characters.

If **m** is zero but **n** is not then an exponential representation is returned where the number of digits of fraction returned is **n**. The form of the fraction is *digit.digits* except when **n** is 1. In this case the output is not a proper representation as the fraction will be of the form ' ' *digit* where the padding space is added due to the absence of a decimal point. For this reason the case **m** = 0, **n** = 1 should not be used in general. When **m** is 0 **string** will contain (**n** + 6) characters for **REALTOSTRING32** and (**n** + 7) for **REALTOSTRING64**.

Each procedure returns a string "**Inf**" preceded by a sign character for infinities and a string "**NaN**" for Not-a-Numbers. In free format a leading space on either string is dropped. Both these will be padded on the right with spaces to fill the field width when free format output is not being used.

Abbreviation An abbreviation specifies a *name* as an *alias* for an existing *element* or for the value of an *expression*. The meaning of the alias is defined by substitution of the abbreviated element or expression.

Actual parameter A parameter used in an *instance* of a procedure.

Alias A name specified by an abbreviation.

Alias check Ensure all elements are identified by a single name within a given *scope*.

Allocation Place a *variable*, *channel*, *timer*, *array* or *port* at an absolute location in memory.

Alternation Combines a number of processes guarded by inputs, and performs the process associated with an input which is ready.

Alternative A component of an *alternation*.

Argument A parameter used in an instance of a function.

Array A number of components of the same type.

Assignment Evaluates an expression or list of expressions, and assigns each result to a corresponding variable.

Bitwise operation Operation on the individual bits in the representation of a value.

Boolean operation Logical evaluation of truth values.

Case input Selects the protocol of an input on a single channel with variant protocol.

Channel Unbuffered, uni-directional point-to-point connection for communication between two processes executing in parallel.

Channel protocol The format of communication on a channel. Communication is valid only if the output and input are compatible; i.e. each communication is of the type specified by the channel protocol.

Choice A component of a conditional.

Communication The communication of values between concurrent processes.

Concurrency Processes acting and existing together.

Conditional A construction (**IF**) which combines a number of processes each of which is guarded by a boolean.

Configuration Configuration associates the components of an occam program with a set of physical resources.

Construction A construction combines processes. occam programs are built from processes, by combining primitive processes and other constructions to form constructions of *sequence* (**SEQ**), *conditional* (**IF**), *selection* (**CASE**), *loop* (**WHILE**), *parallel* (**PAR**) or *alternation* (**ALT**).

Deadlock A state in which two or more concurrent processes can no longer proceed due to a communication interdependency.

Declaration Specifies the name, type and scope of a *variable*, *channel*, *timer* or *array*.

Delayed input A special *timer input* which will wait until the timer has incremented beyond a specified time before terminating. Useful for adding a simple delay in a process.

Element A syntactic structure (a *name*, *subscripted name* or *segment*) which selects *variables*, *channels*, *timers* or *arrays*.

Expression list A list of expressions separated by commas; used in *multiple assignment* and *functions*.

Formal parameter Parameter specified in the definition of a procedure or function. A formal parameter acts as an *abbreviation* for the *actual parameter* used in an *instance* of a procedure.

Free channel A variable whose name is free name.

Free name A name which occurs within a process, but is not specified within the process.

Free variable A variable whose name is a free name.

Function definition Specifies a name for a value process or expression list.

Guard Determines the execution of an associated process in a choice (*boolean guard*) or alternative (*input guard*).

Indentation An offset from the left hand edge of the page. In occam indentation is critical, and serves to define the structure of processes.

Input Receive a value from a channel and assign the value to a variable.

Input guard An input which guards an alternative in an alternation.

Instance The occurrence of a procedure or application of a function.

Invalid process A process whose behaviour has for some reason become undefined, and as a result may lead to the failure of a system. Most invalid processes will be found by the compiler, and may be corrected during program development. The behaviour of an invalid process not detected by the compiler may be set to behave in one of three ways; the process may behave like the primitive process **STOP**, allowing other processes to continue, or the process may cause the whole system to halt, or the process may behave in an undefined way.

Literal A literal is a textual representation of a known value, and has a data type.

Livelock A divergent process, one which remains internally active but does not perform further communication, i.e. it behaves like the following process:
```
WHILE TRUE
  SKIP
```

Modulo operator A modulo operator performs its operation (**PLUS**, **MINUS**, **TIMES**) with no check for overflow. The value returned as a result is the cyclic value within the range of the operand type.

Network a network consists of a number of processing devices, microcomputers perhaps, with the facility to communicate with each other.

Operand Yields a value in an expression.

Operator (monadic or dyadic) performs an operation on its operand(s).

Output Send the value of an expression to a channel.

Placement A configuration statement which places a process on a particular processing device.

Primitive type A primitive type is a channel, timer, integer, boolean, byte or real type. A *port* is also a primitive type.

Priority Priority can be given to a parallel executing on a single processing device. Lower priority processes on such a device may only continue when all higher priority processes are unable to. The inputs which guard alternatives in an alternation may be given a selection priority. If two or more inputs are ready, the the input with the highest priority is selected.

Procedure definition A procedure definition specifies a name for a process.

Procedure instance An instance of a procedure is a use of the procedure, and behaves like a substitution of the process named in the procedure definition. The phrase "procedure call" is used in many other languages, to indicate the use of a procedure, and has a similar meaning. Although the behaviour of an occam procedure is clearly defined as the substitution of the procedure body, a procedure may be implemented as either a substitution or as a call to a closed subroutine.

Process A process starts, performs a number of actions, and then either stops without completing or terminates complete. occam programs are built from the primitive processes *assignment* (:=), *input* (?), *output* (!), **SKIP** and **STOP**. These primitives are combined in **SEQ**, **IF**, **CASE**, **WHILE**, **PAR** and **ALT** constructions.

Protocol The format and *type* of values passed on a channel.

Real time The actual time taken for a physical process to occur.

Relational operation A relational operation compares its operands and yields a boolean result.

Repetitive process A repetitive process (**WHILE**) executes the associated process as long as the specified condition is true; if the condition is initially false the associated process is not executed.

Replication A replicator produces a number of similar components of a construction.

Retyping conversion A retyping conversion changes the data type of a bit pattern, from one data type to another. There are two kinds of retyping conversions: conversions which convert an element, and conversions which convert the value of an expression. Such a conversion has no effect upon the bit pattern, and differs from *type conversion* where the value of one type is represented as an equivalent value of another type.

Scope The region of a program associated with the specification of a name.

Segment A segment is one or more components of an array.

Selection A selection process (**CASE**) executes a process from a list of associated options. The options are selected by matching a selector with a constant expression associated with the option.

Sequence A sequential process (**SEQ**) is one where one action follows another.

Sequential protocol A sequential protocol specifies a sequence of simple protocols as the format of communication on a channel.

Shift operation Perform logical shift of the bit pattern of a value.

Skip Start, perform no action and terminate immediately.

Specification A specification is either a declaration, an abbreviation or a definition and specifies a name which may be used within the associated scope.

Specifier Identifies the type of an *alias* given in an abbreviation or definition.

Stop Start, perform no further action and do not terminate.

String A sequence of ASCII characters equivalent to a table of bytes.

Subscript An expression which selects a component of an array.

Table An array of values of the same type, used in expressions.

Tag Identifier of a protocol variant specified in a *variant protocol* definition.

Timer A timer is a clock which can accessed by any number of concurrent processes.

Timer input A timer input inputs a value from a timer.

Type conversion A type conversion converts the value of an expression of one data type into a similar value of another data type.

Value process A value process produces one or more results, each of primitive data type.

Variable A variable is an element of data type which may be assigned to by input or assignment.

Variable list A list of variables used in a *multiple assignment*.

Variable subscript A variable subscript is a subscript whose value depends on a variable, a procedure parameter, or the index of a replicator with a base or count which is not a constant or constant expression.

Variant protocol Specifies a list of possible protocols for communication on a single channel.

Index